LOVER THROUGH DEPARTURE

NEW AND SELECTED POEMS

ALSO BY RISHMA DUNLOP

Poetry

White Album (2008)
Metropolis (2005)
Reading Like a Girl (2004)
The Body of My Garden (2002)

Drama

The Raj Kumari's Lullaby (Radio Drama, 2005)

As Editor

White Ink: Poems on Mothers and Motherhood (2007)
Red Silk: An Anthology of South Asian Canadian Women Poets (with Priscila Uppal, 2004)

LOVER THROUGH DEPARTURE

NEW AND SELECTED POEMS

Rishma Dunlop

Mansfield Press

Printed in Canada

Library and Archives Canada Cataloguing in Publication

Dunlop, Rishma, 1956-
Lover through departure : new and selected poems / Rishma Dunlop.

ISBN 978-1-894469-56-2

I. Title.

PS8557.U53995L68 2011 C811'.6 C2011-906333-6

Edited by David Sobelman
Design: Denis De Klerck
Cover Photo: Patrick Heagney/iStockphoto
Author Photo: David Spowart

The publication of *Lover Through Departure* has been generously supported by the Canada Council for the Arts and the Ontario Arts Council.

ONTARIO ARTS COUNCIL
CONSEIL DES ARTS DE L'ONTARIO

Canada Council for the Arts
Conseil des Arts du Canada

Mansfield Press Inc.
25 Mansfield Avenue, Toronto, Ontario, Canada M6J 2A9
Publisher: Denis De Klerck
www.mansfieldpress.net

for David Sobelman

CONTENTS

New Poems

The Language of Birds – 13
Lover Through Departure – 14
Birth of a City – 16
Paris – 21
Lisbon – 34
Carson City – 35
July 18 – 36
Signs – 37
September – 38
Ancestors – 40
Girl on the Crowsnest Highway – 42
Beauty – 44
Canto – 46
Recurrence – 47
Little Girl-Deluxe – 48
Dream – 49
Sleep – 50

From ***White Album*** (2008)

Journey to the Dominion of Canada – 53
Vigil for Resident Aliens – 54
Love Field, 1963 – 55
Cherries in the Snow 1968 – 58
Soundtracks – 59
Belle de Jour – 60
Libretto – 61
Adagio – 63
Dream of Billie – 64
Elegy – 65
August Wedding: Anand Karaj – 66
Hush – 69
What Begins Bitterly – 70

Driving Home With Chet – 72
Stop-time – 73
Give Us This Day – 74
Dream of a Little Breakfast – 75
Ain't No Cure – 76

From ***Metropolis*** (2005)

Memory Palace – 79
The New Republic of Letters – 80
Seeing – 82
Testament – 84
Metropolis Redux – 85
Still Life – 96
Dream Sequence When the Moon Is Rising – 97
Psalm – 99
Film Noir – 100
City of Madness and Love – 101

From ***Reading Like a Girl*** (2004)

Let Me Tell You of the Sacred – 105
Gathering Lilacs – 106
Primer – 107
Reading Like a Girl 2 – 110
Reading Like a Girl 3 – 111
Reading Like a Girl 4 – 112
Reading Like a Girl 5 – 113
Reading Like a Girl 6 – 114
Slow Dancing: Beaconsfield 1973 – 115
Somewhere, a Woman is Writing a Poem – 116
Theology – 117
Alphabet – 118

Soja – 119
First Lessons: Postcolonial – 121
Reading Chekhov – 123
Lector in Fabula – 126
Reading Amy Lowell – 127
Benediction – 131
Amas Veritas – 132
Saccade – 133
Retablos – 136
Claim – 137
Cartography – 139
Postscript – 149

From ***The Body of My Garden*** (2002)

Hunger – 145
Montreal – 146
The Art of Travel: A Fable – 148
Prayer – 149
Chahar Bagh: The Four Chambered Garden – 150
Dilkusha: Garden of Heart's Delight – 151
Bagh-I Vafa: Garden of Fidelity – 152
Another Garden: The Seeds of Empire – 153
Stories From Boundary Bay, 1997 – 154
Slippage – 156
Concordance – 157
The Fragrance of Love – 158
Tourniquet – 159

Notes – 161
Acknowledgements – 165

One should say before sleeping, "I have lived many lives. I have been a slave and a prince. Many a beloved has sat upon my knees and I have sat upon the knees of many a beloved. Everything that has shall be again."

—W.B. Yeats

NEW POEMS

THE LANGUAGE OF BIRDS

This morning I woke to blackbirds singing
a multitude waiting for me to bless.

This morning I wonder if St. Francis was right—
if Perfect Joy can only be found nailed to the Cross.

This morning I know the love we cling to—
and the constant fear we'll lose our grip.

This morning, if I could preach to birds
I'd tell them—fly and kiss, lives depend on this.

LOVER THROUGH DEPARTURE

1

Talk of death unhinges me.
My sentinel—vigilant over my sleep.

In your bed, I hold fast against the dispensation
of your faith, your root insistence on the soul's

demand. I'm not convinced, until you request
I surrender my will to be cremated—
to bend our bodies—bone to bone
in a single grave.

2

Your beta-blockers and blood-thinners
the cocked barrel of death so near—

popped at timed intervals—you
never imagined living long enough to meet me.

3

While you sleep, I lay my head against
your heart's arterial rage—

listen to its faulty hammer,
the night collared in my mouth.

4

It's been a long time since I slept
in the tenderness of someone's breath.

If I touch you now, you'll wake to
a storybook moon over Superstition Freeway

and you'll rise naked over palms and cacti
along the road, above the rooftops like thunder.

5

I dream of you through all my departures—
through hunger and love and outrage.

It stuns me—
like the astonishment of white dahlias

releasing their clipped hours of autumn—
as our bodies begin the slow dissolve

and I feel you—like a homecoming—
bone to bone in a single grave.

BIRTH OF A CITY

1

The choice of the site is a serious matter. The fate of our people depends on it. Gods of the city, reveal your will through the oracle's words, through the flight of a bird, through the flow of the wind, through sacrifice, through nature's signs.

Our town is seen in the eyes of a crow,
fixed on future skyscrapers, bus terminals,
markets, gardens, garbage dumps.

Ordained to face northwest, off the lake,
at the water's edge, where plateaus drain the ocean,
there, I see our site's lay of the land.

We dream a place opening on the world.
Among those who have arrived, I witness
our muffled emergencies. Music of weariness

slams our days. Eardrums burst and deafness
numbs. Someone's heart about to stop. Someone's
about to break a leg. Someone's about to be delivered.

Someone's seeking redemption. Tiny skulls
recite, on sedimentary rock, psalms of gardens
and serpents and apple tragedies.

But such prayers exhaust, till I see the crow
weep for us, take the blame for us. He travels
upwards, black turning white, white turning yellow,

wings about to crash into the moon. Yellow turning red,
as it veers into a hawkish stance, and turns into a dancer.
Circling his mate, he seduces her.

She spreads her legs, and an angel comes
to expel them from paradise, caring nothing
for the mating song and dance, he ferries them

to the night watchman. Wings outstretched
in longing, I turn and make my way,
nailing heaven and earth together.

Blackbird and lover are one in the flicker
of the future, centuries imagined in memory's
furious history, ardent with expectation.

2

—fixing the region, naming its landmarks

Slow flapping in sunset's copper, two torn ribbons
fly over rain-glossed fields. The crow's shadow rakes
the ground below, turns the sky into a vault of heaven.

Black trees knife into a tattoo of stars.
In its homing, I am adrift, a black mote moving
across the evening to join my murder,

perched, to overview the site from the roost
of the alders, their massive, shifting shades,
mortal roots gone down in darkness.

3

—raising a sacred enclosure

In euphony, the crow takes dead branches
back to emptiness, entwines twigs into the limbs
of a tree of life, with wild, unfailing patience.

Till what was fallen and lost is reborn, and incapable
of recovering the past. We are ready to take a place in its nest,
our new city born of blood sacrifice and dreams.

Morning rises in the blackbird's beak, aimed
full-target at the heart of the sun. But the sun only
brightens and darkens and I smell the day,

dried blood turning fragrant, placental sweetness,
vaguely familiar, as my eye cuts the land, like a crow,
divining pleasure, foreseeing the public heart.

4

—surveying the four directions, I stand, I sit, I kneel—I lie down

I kiss the ground, my nostrils flared with the scent
of afterbirth. I see the crow is a childhood story,
a legend, a totem, a fable, a trickster,

an outsider, an omen, a knave. Four and twenty crows
must be baked in a pie, a dainty dish for a king.
His six-sided bedtime song of presage and rhyme.

5

—assess the site by the rules of the science of augury

I gesture to the field of view with my knotless staff,
forbidden to draw divining lines by hand alone.
I must trust the crow and my divine wand and labours

of the tongue, mouths opened full into lyric
by charred war memories when our oracle spoke
of our loss, rage, fury, exile. And the site, found

by parting the human dark to the harbour, empties
into beauty, naming things into knowledge,
dictating where souls will reside in these sloping hills.

6

—announce the three, the three names every city must have

The priestly, first, where trees meet the water.
The public's then, to gather in the meeting place.
And the secret, sacred name, Fortitude.

7

—draw the place, sky, ground and underground

In the intercession of signs and symbols, the crow joins
the temple watchers, the guardian gazes of angels
and gargoyle muses. Watching crow caw the sounds

of dim battalions, my eyes are shell-shocked.
I open them to revelation, a bird's-eye view
that sees through the portholes of creation.

to a theory of beauty, flaunted through the vernal
explosion of spring, the layout of the city's
foundation and the Dog Star in a baroque sky

and the quartered circle, divine enclosure, our oracle
of belonging, a heaven. We are surprised, caught off guard.
His augury has located our place. He draws a map,

naming our covenant. Lessons of scriptures and physics
show us unweathered thresholds. We find our life
in this landscape, chart the grids and people, the site

with the city's true body of human faces as the mind,
the old crow, seeks to read the signs. We shall be
what we know, brains in wings and hands,

the city itself, eternal, imprinted on its inauguration, living
through winds, bombs, ruins, restorations,
the fact of us, human visitors, fleshly, fleeting.

PARIS

Air Canada Flight 880 Toronto to Paris. Child's city of miniatures, tin-foil glint in dawn blue as fragile as aerogrammes. Eros in the lick of envelope strips, in the sealing. I read *Emily L.* by Marguerite Duras. You wait for me in a small hotel on the Left Bank. The fume and roar of landing. The grind of wheels extending. I cannot remember your eyes, their colour. Time's strange torque flames against my ear.

May 7

First day. We make it last as long as possible—to enter Paris time. Bistro lunch near The Sorbonne. *Café crème, salade niçoise, un verre.* Sun cracks the pavement, cross-hatches the asphalt with wicker chairs, every one of us watching the street.

It's my first time in Paris. You want to take me to Café de Flore. De Beauvoir wrote entire novels here. The café is brimming with tourists. I think of Georges Perec, and his attempt to exhaust a Parisian ambience. For three days in October 1974, he sat in cafés around the Place St. Sulpice, jotting down what remains unremarkable, a dull list: *The bells stop ringing (is it vespers?). A 63 bus goes by almost empty. Night, winter: unreal aspect of the passers-by. A man carrying carpets on his shoulders.*

Years ago, in a university course on experimental fiction, I read a Perec novel. He wrote it without ever using the letter "e." Difficult to do with the French language. On my bookshelf, a tattered copy of Perec's *Life: A User's Manual* about dozens of interconnected lives in a Paris apartment block.

At Bistro des Augustins, sourdough *pain Poilâne,* runny cheeses. Back at the tiny hotel, a tiny room. Your body smells like rain. Sleep-curved into the big mitt of your chest, your mouth pressed to my ear.

Vertigo as you give me your unpublic face. The mesh and slur of zippers. The fricative click of throat and tongue. Love arrives in a carnal burlesque of many mouths—thunder perfect.

* * *

Reading in the blue hour of morning. Duras' words: *I told you I loved you. You never answered such insane talk.* I place the book on the nightstand with the silver O of the bracelet you gave me.

* * *

Since girlhood, I had thought of the love affair as a work of art. My parents watching the film *A Man and a Woman.* Anouk Aimée's shock of black hair sweeping across her eyes, in bed smoking with her lover. She says *I am married.*

When I am older and watch it again, late at night while my husband and daughter are sleeping, I realize that she is a widow and her beloved husband, the movie stuntman, is dead.

Despite being widowed, she struggles with betrayal, grief—the sensibility of adultery that is so alive in her. *How I longed for that kind of romance.*

I like the French lover in the Citroën who has a conscience about "the affair"; he doesn't push her. How I wished for the final scene at the train station set to Francis Lai's soundtrack.

Years later, I think of this film again, as I sit in a lover's bed. He brushes my hair from my eyes and I watch him smoke a cigarette before I drive home on the freeway to return to my husband and child.

May 8

Paris is for *les amoureux.* In the *sixième,* the Jardin du Luxembourg, a young woman straddles the lap of her lover, kissing. *Il y a des baisers partout.*

Children sail miniature toy boats in the pond surrounded by statues of French queens. They ride the merry-go-round and watch the puppet theatre.

Everywhere in this park, uniformed gardeners stand guard. Each tree carefully espaliered—the permitted forms: bobbin, pyramid, palm, double U. One of the gardeners tells us we could take twenty free lessons on the pear tree and its enemies.

On the surrounding walls, a photography exhibition by Reporters Without Borders, *sans frontières.* Images of starving bellies of skeletal children. A burka-clad woman points a pistol at an enemy we can't see—just out of the sightline of the photograph.

May 9, morning

I had forgotten your architect's eyes. How I loved it when we first met, and I wrapped my tongue and eyes around the language of ornament, the egg and dart borders, the Mansard roofs, the carved stone acanthus leaves you showed me. Here on the Rue des Bons Enfants: a perfect cartouche.

You teach me to think through cities, through maps and grids, buildings and sculptures, the concentric circles of *arrondissements.* You show me the places on public statues where the patina has been rubbed shiny by passing hands. A woman's breast, Montaigne's shoe.

* * *

You are the consummate married lover. My abandonment to you was complete. I wanted your mind—the way your words made love to me as surely as your hands. What I wanted most was your mouth. To be swallowed whole, where body and language meet. To enter the gateways of the body and to be consumed.

* * *

A little girl walks by hand in hand with her mother and I flash back to my husband and daughter. She is about five years old dressed in her red wool coat with the velvet collar, her grey-suited father clasping her hand. The image of my husband stroking our daughter's hair, reaching down for her, an image I claim as love. When she was a baby, spit out from between my legs, how we loved her. He changed her diapers. Even the shit didn't matter. He would wipe clean the tender folds of her vulva, powder her, wrap her in a blanket. And then there is another image of the three of us standing hand in hand, an enduring snapshot of elegance.

May 9, midnight

We meet the photographer at Parc Lafayette for drinks and dinner at an African restaurant in the 11th *arrondissment,* Equatore. My tongue explodes with pineapple, coconut, pomegranate spiked with lime and habanero chile, ginger drink, plantain fried sweet, and fish, and rice. The photographer buys me jasmine flowers from the yellow-toothed vendor who approaches the tables. The gift annoys you.

Later, at Le Chat Noir. The photographer orders me a Calvados—hot transfusion of apple. Over his armagnac, the photographer smokes a cigar. He tells me his story, how he was struck by lightning one night a few years ago. It changed everything. His sense of smell, taste, the sensations of sex.

Back at the hotel, the scent of jasmine overpowers the small room. You discard the bouquet but the fragrance rises, swallows the bed with its sting.

May 10

Left Bank café. Gertrude Stein's still tender buttons on a dress of lilies. Bistro chairs capable of playing Mozart.

Translation

Monday	=	Soir bleu
Mardi	=	Delirium
Wednesday	=	Place de la Concorde
Jeudi	=	Winged Victory
Friday	=	Merde

* * *

Thinking about love affairs in films. Richard Gere and Diane Lane in *Unfaithful*. The married woman buys new black lingerie for her lover. I'm with her, snipping the tags of the black lace bra. It's not so much that the marriage bed is boring, it's just that it is well-worn, known territory, devoid of astonishment. The lover can be approached with abandonment, lust, language—the body becomes new and young again.

May 11

Musée d'Orsay. The girders of the old railway station, statues by Rodin, paintings by Delacroix, Ingres, Seurat, Gauguin.

Louis Vins Restaurant for dinner.

In the beginning—spark and fever. Ridges of muscle and pulse. Your perfect juncture of clavicle and shoulder. Each time we broke each other. Faint, implausible dreams. My hand followed your ribs to rupture.

Stunned that no great complaints or dissatisfaction were essential to adultery. Bones of our marriages still intact, a door opened and we entered. You kissed my earlobe, unfastened my earrings. A new city spread wide before us in tremor.

May 12

The crowds at the Tuileries and the Luxembourg are a contrast to the Bois du Boulogne. Here, the Parc de Bagatelle sweeps us back in time. Once the château of the Marquis of Hertford, its style is still English, abundant rose gardens, strutting peacocks. Along the tree-shaded paths we find the orangerie, where a cellist plays under the stars.

May 13

The photographer keeps calling. Wants to see me again before we leave Paris. You are irritated but you owe him for some past favour so we meet him in the Marais. Every narrow street yields private courtyards hidden behind number-coded entry doors. During the day, some occupants leave the security codes off and we are able to explore these inner worlds by simply pressing the entry buttons.

We shop on Rue de Rosiers, buy falafel and bread, containers of red peppers, taramasalata with dill, aubergines, poppy seed bagels. We take our feast to the apartment of an independent filmmaker who has just finished wrapping a new movie. He tells me this is his pied-à-terre away from his wife and child. The lesbian slasher B-movie he directed was filmed here. They had just cleaned up the fake blood on the white painted floor before we arrived.

May 14

Montparnasse cemetery. Sartre and de Beauvoir are buried together. It surprises me. I see the stone that marks Baudelaire's bones.

I am more interested in the grave that belongs to Serge Gainsbourg. Shrine of flowers, Métro tickets, photographs. At Rue de Verneuil, hundreds of messages graffiti the gates and walls of his house. The interior, shared with Jane Birkin for years, was painted black. Gainsbourg died March 2, 1991, in his bed, but I still hear him, *l'enfant terrible,* alcohol-soaked and nicotine-stained, singing and panting with Jane through "Je T'aime...Moi Non Plus."

At Brancusi's statue, "Le Baiser," a young man asks me to join him for a glass of wine. I tell him I am a tourist, that you are waiting for me.

May 15

This is a city of public kissing and lovers' trysts. Under the iconic shadow of Robert Doisneau's "The Kiss at l'Hôtel de Ville," the James Deanish rumple-haired young man with the remains of his cigarette between thumb and fingers once postered my teenage bedroom. We've all seen the young woman he is kissing, 1950s refined, twin-setted, but her head is thrown back with such passion that we can't help but get swept into the embrace.

I am reading a book on the subject of the public kiss: *Où s'embrasser à Paris.* The guidebook provides addresses suitable for the act of kissing, a series of symbols for each site, the most romantic time of the day, the best time of the year, and whether kisses should be long or discreet. The first chapter, titled "*Les grands classiques,*" includes Doisneau's famous kissing site, but explains that to precisely replicate that kiss, your lips should meet at the Café de l'Hôtel de Ville at the table directly under the letter "C" of Café.

Another *classique* is the Pont-Neuf, the city's most popular suicide location.

The guidebook also mentions the tree-shaped Place de Furstenberg on the Left Bank as a perfect, quiet spot for a long embrace after hours at the cafés de Flore and Deux Magots. The book recommends that you remain standing while kissing. Kissing that enters all the gateways of the body. Your mouth is where body and language meet.

On a wall at the bookstore, I read Lorca's words

The still waters of your mouth
in a thicket of kisses

May 16

Markets ripen with cheeses and foie-gras. Bouquets of field flowers. You admire my newly purchased stilettos. The surprise of it, how I like it when the deep South and the brokedown rivers of your childhood inflect your speech, when you dub me *doll-face*. When you ask for affection, *gimme some shuggah*.

May 17

At the abbey in St. Germain, we see where Descartes is buried. His head was stolen from a burial place in Stockholm, travelled widely until it was finally reunited with his body.

Paris feeds my appetite for words. The place names taste like food. The lion fountains outside L'Église Saint Sulpice. In the Chappelle des Saint Anges, the Delacroix frescoes, Jacob's half-nelson with the devil. La Chappelle de la Vierge. Homage à Marie Immaculée.

Sompteuse.

May 18

The Louvre. Hours in the Denon wing. Crowds line up in front of *Mona*, groups of Japanese schoolgirls in blue uniforms, throngs on Da Vinci Code tours, tattered copies of Dan Brown's novel in hand.

Near Rue du Faubourg St. Honoré, the famous Ladurée for late tea and pastries. The green and gold canopied shop was built in 1862, with ceilings of badly executed cupids, walls mirrored and gilded. You are uncomfortable here among the ladies of a certain age, gilded and Guccied. The waitresses serve in frilly pinnies: pastries, éclairs, tarts with glazed fruits, *tarte aux poireaux*. Pink and pistachio macaroons, mille-feuille. On the marble-topped tables, tea leaves in silver pots.

In the window, an almost full-size chocolate bust of Marie Antoinette, head coiffed with meringues and roses for hair, a bustier of macaroons.

* * *

Fidelity. Stanley Kubrick's *Eyes Wide Shut*. The husband, played by Tom Cruise, confronts his wife, played by Nicole Kidman, asks half jokingly if she has any fantasies and is stunned when she responds with a full-blown erotic scene involving a naval officer. Cruise then turns to the titillation of the orgies of an occult sect where there is ultimately no morality, no marriage, yet the password is *fidelio*.

May 19

Tour Eiffel. Kafka warned against the heaven reaching tower. But here, everyone is a cliché of the hopeless romantic. In the chain of desire, I want to believe in what we shelter in the salt of our hands.

(Last night I dreamed that your face was smooth, lipless, a mouth not yet cut. That we could no longer kiss while making love.)

May 20

We laugh when I read you the excerpt from a food guide published by French *Vogue*. A new section is titled "Restaurants with Flattering Light." The restaurant Benoît is cited as having "a quality of light particularly adapted to beauties in the style of Emma Bovary." The Chanel bag-sized guide includes places to avoid during a *liaison dangereuse*.

* * *

Paris is perfume. Nostalgia for mother's dressing table. Evening in Paris. Bottles of Caron's Fleurs de Rocaille and Worth's Je Reviens. Deneuve's impeccable face in ads for Chanel No. 5. Yves Saint Laurent's Rive Gauche. Guerlain's Vetiver. L'Heure Bleue. Bottles of Nahema on Deneuve's dressing table. Her perfect maquillage—cinematic, striding Paris streets in her buckled Vivier pumps.

The writer I knew who died of cancer, a beautiful woman whose signature scent had been made for her in Grasse. Fields of Centifolia roses. The scents of alleys—piss and booze and food—Moroccan scents of orange water, mint and tea.

* * *

Bastille Métro to Promenade Plantée in the 12th. A garden built into an unused railway viaduct, vintage 1859. Lavender, roses, a profusion of verdure and trees—cherry, lime, maple. Rose-laden bowers against the railway arches and brickwork. Buff male joggers saturated with aftershave.

From the walkway, we see the streets lined with *belle époque* apartment buildings. We are voyeurs, peering into people's lives. In the Viaduc des Arts, artists make and restore violins, restore ancient maps, restore paintings on canvas.

May 21

Arab quarter. We eat spicy Merguez sausage, duck tagine, fish couscous. You tell me about an article in *Le Monde,* about Arab boys burning cars with gasoline. The mothers of Clichy-sous-Bois remembering the riots of 2005. In the Muslim ghettos, bleak concrete high-rises, children who have given up on the May '68 revolution. They want jobs. They want security. Sarkozy's threat to "karcherize" the ghettos of "*la racaille,*" to blast them with high-pressure water hoses—washing away the scum off the streets like pigeon shit. The Imams cannot help. The mothers believed children born in France would be *citoyens.* Amidst the pimps and hashish dealers, the Parisian-born boys swagger in nicked gold chains, cell phones in hand, unable to find work—their five-digit postal codes ratting them out. The suburbs of Paris—burning.

May 22

The photographer told us to try a Hammam. Across the road from the Jardin des Plantes. We walk through the giant arched doorway, entering a decadent 1920s Marrakesh, the Hammam de la Mosquée. Today is for women only. We agree to meet later and I enter deep secret chambers tiled in green, blue, and gold. Silence syncopated by a trickle of water from a fountain.

Enter the labyrinth, structured like the interior of a pyramid, antechamber leading into antechamber to the heart—the steam room.

A cream marble room with turquoise mosaic pillars. Arched windows let in shafts of sunlight above the steam. Six alcoves of marble platforms reveal dim outlines of naked women sweating. Occasionally, they douse themselves with cold water but there is a sense of complete languor.

After the steam, a plunge into icy water closes my pores. I walk weak-kneed to the massage room, lie back on pillowed platforms. Above, a ceiling of gold, green, and red. Around me, carved pillars, exquisitely painted panels, prone women: beautiful, ordinary, tiny, gigantic. A strong sensation of being in a harem, and the expectation that, at any moment, eunuchs will emerge around us.

The masseuse goes about her business with a slap of oil. Around me, French women compare anti-cellulite creams, face masks, the latest cosmetics. The voyeur in me takes strange satisfaction from the large, slack-fleshed women secretly emerging from their perfectly coutured outfits.

My final recovery from metropolitan stress takes place outside the Hammam in the Moorish courtyard of the mosque. Amidst a profusion of roses, trees, small round mosaic-inlaid café tables, I order sweet mint tea. Waiters offer trays of pastries filled with honey and dates. In a glass case there are squares of Turkish Delight, lemon and rose-water slabs the size of bricks. Behind the mosque is the Place du Puits-de-l'Ermite, an enclave tiled in green with carved doors and pink marble fountains.

Historical irony in contemporary France. This compound, devoted to religion and pleasure, was built as a gesture of gratitude by the French in 1926, for the North Africans who fought in the First World War.

May 23

Last night. Les Bouquinistes restaurant for dinner. I'm learning to eat prawns the French way, with heads still attached.

The city, a wrecked nightclub chanteuse, sounds its own rung music. There is an ache in the molars of the Métro. Keen. Persistent. I realize your eyes are grey. I call out your name. The sound I make sounds like Paris.

Love is to imagine, to be complicit with distance. Paul Éluard writes *I speak to you across cities...My mouth is upon your pillow.*

In Paris, the smell of rain-slick streets was narcotic, a mineral swarm that clung to us, our flame visible under pink-fisted trees as the night hours bent and laid us down.

* * *

LISBON

Waiting for you in the square—a singer beckoned me.
I followed her shadow along the stone walls
of the deserted abbey near the Tejo River,
as she sang her *fado*. I took my religion from the city,
on a night when I was poured out like water.

We slept holding each other's hands
in Stevens' paradise of imperfections, hot with
flawed and stubborn sounds, replete with dreams
of miracles—like a scene from *The Godfather*—
you tore off my feathered dress, releasing a flock of doves.

CARSON CITY

Air violet over the mesa and
music leaking from the rental car
merge with the tire's drone on the highway,
and a country song, pain-drenched in three-quarter time.
A cheerful heartbreak
drawling a dreary affair: hypnotic, hilarious.

We glide along in the moment, still, silent, suspended
in the moving car—minds clear-sighted about how little
there is to say—we bob our heads to the cheatin' and
hurtin' waltz, and hear the engine pull a dare—
for the room at the desert motel where we shall ache
to be taken all ways at once.

JULY 18

for Rachel

I heard the lifting of eyelids,
saw the blue of your temples,
and reached out at dawn—

when I saw you torn from me
I saw you in your own death
and in mine,

and that moment of your birth
unsealed the house of memory
and became all our remembered hours.

They go with me in the endless, measureless light,
like the songs I sang to you—songs heard in the
winds and lakes and rivers of your childhood,

heard in the days I walked you to school,
syncopated by your skipping and singing—
red-ribboned ponytail slapping the morning air

and the slap, slap of sockeyed salmon
swimming upstream to spawning beds,
heard in your mother's voice

that delivers you to the possible
everywhere,
like a cross above your bed.

SIGNS

Some days, in an unlit room, I still see my classmates and me writing in lined notebooks, autograph books, and high school yearbooks, our fingers tracing the embossed typography of The Beatles' *White Album*, white-on-white letters, and our crude hearts, gushing initials, proclaiming the loves we carved on schoolyard oaks—the scars of language in English Quebec—when our signs were X'd out with black paint and words like STOP were replaced by ARRÊT.

I still feel the first time I touched a Braille reader, or the raised impasto of an oil painting, and sensed that pain and pleasure can be read, like signs in the city: *The Cool Hand of a Girl Coffee Shop, Shalom Shanghai*, the tattoo of a newspaper, date, masthead, headline and all on a commuter's arm or the graffiti above a viaduct—*I love you. Fuck death.*

I still remember the time when I first touched you—Churchill gone to his grave, ban lifted on *Lady Chatterley's Lover*, The Beatles performing "Twist and Shout" at Shea Stadium, Jacqueline Dupré shaking the dust off Elgar.

How thirsty I was. Everything I touched rose up in sparks. Even the side-walks sang the carnal drift of things. I wanted to always keep that wild honey in my hands. But the signs changed, and your lips no longer left traces on my forehead, only the ruin of astonishment, and I remained vigilant, reading the signs.

SEPTEMBER

September, grazed with TV euphemisms, scorched our brains with the doused smell of charred towers. I remember the phone ringing and my husband saying *I'm coming home.*

I imagine him leaving his office, striding back towards us through smoke and fuselage and dissonance, as the baby moves from sleep to singing between her crib bars.

I made coffee—an act of faith. The first cup dark and necessary. Around me the sky gone crazy with fear and the spew of glass and steel, and the morning was born of my hand with a bitter taste.

The phone rings again, and I imagine your voice calling me. Years since I last saw you, the path between us almost bricked up. *I needed to hear your voice* you say. I imagine phones ringing across the city, lovers who had lost each other, calling out to each other, finding each other again. In my dreams I often hear you calling my name. I imagine us drinking coffee, during our mornings of stolen hours, and the skyline just beyond the terrace covered in translucent voile curtains.

Your voice enters me like a lozenge of heat, stalled in my throat like a drop of blood on a glass slide. I'm astonished by the blow of memory, how my departures and returns don't weaken with age, how lips to flesh remind me of the moment next to death. And the scorched city spreads before us, flaring against a carbon-choked sky.

I imagine your grin, unclamped from your final howl, hear the fear in your voice, not from terror or bombs, but from something ravelled out of sound—severed—like an amputated limb. Whatever words we say, in the end, are disconsolate, goodbyes swallowed into the dial tone of bruises and ruin as I set the phone down in its cradle. I never told you *the baby has your eyes.*

Night cameras trained on the nerve sockets of a nation. In the hum of the wound, you come back through the flame pit of the dead, fingers reaching out like stems of flowers. I didn't weep for you at first, but the day after, my ears to the lips of the dying, in a Manhattan dawn, with the morning newspaper, and a violinist on the front page playing Barber's Adagio, tears cutting tracks into my face.

I wept in a silence that would not leave me alone, for your body that is mine, for the eyes that are yours, walking out of the soot-lined hours, our dreams slipping in rivers of ash, as the roses in the garden unleash their red fury into the dark.

ANCESTORS

I hear them behind me in another continent
across the Indian Ocean,
soft sweep of sandals crossing the floors

in my mother's country. I was born there
decades ago at 2 A.M. My birth certificate reads
One Living Female Child.

My mother's land is still there,
scooters and rickshaws in crowded streets,
billboards of light-skinned Bollywood starlets,

and Lakmé Fairever Fairness face cream,
dreamscapes of lotus ponds,
lush public gardens, the smells of decay and jasmine,

rivers marking the routes of cranes and egrets,
in bustling bazaars and stinking alleyways,
cities like Victorian London among palm trees and banyans.

The ancestors are still there, watching the officers of
the British Raj in the white pavilioned days,
the swill and clink of quinine and tanqueray

echoing across the hillside stations and their railways
across the bloodied border of Kashmir and
the births of midnight's children.

The ancestors are still there, drinking chai with cardamom
widows in white saris, turbaned sirdars,
the young women with amber skin, hair and brows as black

as crows' wings, eyes of lionesses in heat,
dressed in silks of delirious hues, violent pinks,
bangles and anklets clinking,

they wander through mirrored rooms
in the last daylight of the century,
painting their eyes with kohl,

brush of sandalwood across the collarbone.
Somewhere out of them, alive or dead I have sprung.
Yet no one seems to recognize me.

No one.

GIRL ON THE CROWSNEST HIGHWAY

She drives into the sky above the Okanagan Valley, cuts the wheels of her father's Silverado into mountain rock and avalanche zones, drives the road where every bend is the brink of nightmare. Black ice everywhere. Winter-locked, she imagines sliding across the edges of cliffs, into glacial lakes.

Past the sign for Hope: *Gateway to Holidayland,* a truck stop and roadside coffee shop reaches for her. She orders her grilled cheese at the diner, listens to the French fries spattering in grease. The man behind the counter cradles them in Styrofoam, looks at her and says: *Storm warning. Where you headed?* The men look her right through and she wonders what family tragedy she could invent for them. Sick mother. Dead lover. Heart trouble.

Back on the road, on the radio, the only channel she gets is country and western. Dwight Yoakum singing Elvis' *Suspicious Minds: I'm caught in a trap, I can't walk out.*

Shadow Lake Reserve. A wolf stands sentinel on the ridge above Manning Park. A white tailed deer runs across her vision. She drives on, listening to the radio, sees the yellow signs with the black crow, Number 3 Crowsnest Highway, and she enters the Fraser Valley across the Skagit River. Signs for Hell's Gate and the RV parks, the Comfort Inn. The sign for Bridal Falls across from the billboard for Hooters restaurant in Vancouver.

She drives on. Her hands, tense on the wheel, undo her every day; like Penelope, she unravels.

Slap of windshield wipers. Wind-stung, she knows that the air is not neutral. Dusk thickens on the fretworks of trees that sag, fresh-weighted with snow like a cheap glossy Christmas card. The moon is worn thin, hauled up like a broken whetstone.

Superstitious girl, she has no faith in templed offerings, or in palms pressed together in prayer. But on the highway she prays to Santa Rita of Cascia, patron saint of the impossible, imagines herself scattering rose petals on every inch of the dead-winter road she claims as home. In the engine hum, so much tenderness composed and savaged, so much that can't bring itself to wake.

So much plot left behind. Photographs and concert tickets wedged into corners of the vanity. Prom dresses and cigarettes smoked in the 7-Eleven parking lot. Above it, her childhood ceiling of glow-in-the dark stars. Her father's whiskey breath.

Just the road now. Nosing to the sky. Chapel-quiet.

BEAUTY

for Cara

Yes, we were young and beautiful
with our noble exhaustion

pushing our strollers and our futures
to school in orchard country, the season

clocked forward by harvests of cherries,
in the arms of the valley,

roads crackling with sagebrush and desert drought.

And the days were also beautiful:
the old steam paddle ship moored in the lake,

the vineyard tours and Happy Hours
at the beachside diner and bar.

Ours was a small town—a summer town—
traffic stopped to let Canada Geese and families

of quail bob across the road.

The high school advertised the prom band—
The Peachland Rollers.

Summer and the living was easy—
your father and I were in love,

hungry for plum kisses among the Ponderosa pines,
sealing the hours under our roof of stars,

where light reads like a fable.

And you were my beauty, my daughter—
you and your sister bikinied poolside,

laughing with your cans of Coke
about how things were—

Ferris wheel turning in the Conklin fair,
your long limbs running for the lake,

hitting the water to cool the heat
of your body chasing beauty

for which we had no words.

CANTO

I never learned the patience to play
the lessons my mother drove me to.

Between my rushed attempts across the keys
the woman upstairs waited for spaces

to play. It's love I feel, not for her
that woman behind plaster who never whispers

a word to her neighbours. But for her fingers
wringing the cello's neck.

RECURRENCE

A girl is walking along Naramata Road. It is my daughter, it is me, arms outstretched, crows rising from her fingertips, a rush of wings above her head. The road stretches through vineyards, around a lake. Sometimes I am my daughter. Sometimes the idea of her. Her hands pluck passing leaves. In the shadow of the valley the leaves are pages torn from the books of the dead. The land yields its particular shining—sweet water and sage, tinderbox waiting for a spark to incinerate.

LITTLE GIRL-DELUXE

She dreams of Coney Island cotton candy, limousine
chauffeured divas. Wakes early, to dim plaster walls,

Harlem echoes of a child's patty-cake game. Walks to
school, streets of magnolias opening and destroying

themselves, over and over. No angels above the tenements,
or in the five-and-dime windows— but on the billboards,

lipsticked women pout. The larger-than-life Chanel model
whispers *Share the fantasy.*

Sarah Jessica Parker in pink evening dress, diamond-glinted lobes,
pushes a new perfume called *Lovely* through Manhattan smog.

The girl looks up at the actress, at her pearl-ringed hands,
hears the gospel sung from the mouths of advertisements—

tries to unglue words from the sky. Memorizes the city
anthems, her brow rinsed with dreams.

DREAM

I'm playing piano in an empty room
even though I never learned to play well—
it's a heavy love, not a soft solo
this music, and I can't stop playing
for the broken bones of Victor Jara—
a kind of madness brought home,
dreamt, until his hands are cut off.

SLEEP

Think of the body's last years—the cage of pain it can be.
Fisted soft as felt in the gloam and hush of cabinet dust,
we're never free of history, the soured ghosts of blood

click and cuff the night, the city's howl coils us in, scrapes
the circuitry of seam-split love. Outside—the world is
gutted and stuffed, gust-tangled.

I fear the cold slab, but you believe the earth has a taste for us,
ridge of gum and bone splinter—you want our bodies there,
close, close—all things open here as you sleep, ears drummed

in your skull's kilter and sag, recall of molar grind in your mouth.
My dream strains to reach you, to lay itself along the length of us.
The body's tether is tenuous—a frail strip of hide.

This—our last stretch of cherried days, my love, and it burns me—
this flamed threnody under the skin, clear and muscular like the flow
of water, bearing us up to a new country, the sky taking us—lifting us

home to one more sleep. Think of it—what has been between
lovers—fire we didn't see coming. To ask for more is an impossible
proposal. I plead for nothing.

WHITE ALBUM
2008

JOURNEY TO THE DOMINION OF CANADA

In the aftermath of the empire's death—
trains cross the border between Pakistan and India,
spilling the severed hands of Sikhs, Hindus, Muslims.

Mother escapes with what she could carry
across the split world from Lahore,
as Kashmir becomes Partition's open sore.

In the aftermath of my birth,
my first days lit by bulbs of white jasmine,
the world spread wide before my parents.

They took what was at hand, father's scientific journals,
mother's gold, her silks and rose-strewn shawls—
they packed their bags, read the guidebooks,

and followed the lines that lead us
from the warm palm of empire
to its furthest frost-bitten fingertips.

VIGIL FOR RESIDENT ALIENS

Thousands cross borders—
each late arrival a ceremony

to announce how far they've travelled.
Language a bruise, roots in parcels,

the smell of miles on their clothes—
countless white nights of insomnia

that kept the roofs from falling.
Citizens become aliens.

Women's veils become partitions.
Turbaned men drive taxis,

English a raw triangle of verbs
in their thick accents—

not my parents' Queen's English.
Passports are fingered nervously

with every border crossing,
every honour killing

of some disobedient bride.
Imagine then,

a descant,
a glass of cool water,

quiet.

LOVE FIELD, 1963

As usual, father woke me
for the daily ritual that required
each of us to grip one end
of starched burgundy muslin
and stretch until, satisfied, he
folded the lengths up and tied
the newly made (like magic) turban
round his long black hair,
then kissed me on the forehead, there,
then disappeared briefcase in hand
out the front door.

On school holidays
I loved to visit him at work,
which was Ayerst Laboratories
with the beakers and all
the way downtown by train,
and how he would have me shrieking
when he flicked that gleaming
pink liquid at my blouse—
the stuff that vanished
like stains in Cheer commercials.

That morning, though,
I dressed myself in my uniform,
packed my book bag,
and went sighing to school,
my nose in *Charlotte's Web*,
as mother planned dinner
with recipes from *Good Housekeeping*.

When I came home, I found her
in the family room ironing,

and watching TV, and ironing.
This soap was new, not *As the World*
Turns, but the woman beside herself
with a bouquet of roses, beside her
husband in the Lincoln
moving past the Texas School Book
Depository to Dealey Plaza, Dallas.
On the black-and-white screen,
the newscaster tells us her suit is pink,
the roses are red. She smiles under her
pillbox hat, waves a white-gloved hand,
in the open motorcade,
then the gunshots,
and the scene replayed.

I realized mother was crying
her whole chest heaving,
something I'd never seen before
and it scared me. I was seven years old
and wanted it to stop,
this weeping that was large and lungful.

That's how father found us in the family room,
amidst mother's ironing,
her pink slip and pedal pushers and pink sari,
her Maidenform girdles and bras,
the pink sleeveless dress and matching coat
she bought me at Ogilvy's Department Store,
all that pink scattered on our floor
and spattered on the floor of the Lincoln
and the TV still going.

Father put his briefcase down
and mother held him
and was held by him.

That night, while the white chalk of hopscotch
games ghosted the streets,
my parents watched the evening news before bed
as was their custom. And they are still there
in the hours before midnight—
the woman with her husband
in his casket at Love Field Airport,
still in the spatter of her pink suit
like the day we did paints in Mrs. Simon's class,
her stockings and her right glove caked
a darker shade.

CHERRIES IN THE SNOW 1968

When my parents go out,
I reach into mother's
bureau drawer,
the top one,

as tall as me,
and wind myself in the white
silk scarf father bought her in Paris,
and roll on her Revlon Cherries

in the Snow lipstick.
Then, I dab perfume on strap lines
that cut across my skin

like trails of Voodoo fighters
curving away from the cauterized part of Viet Nam
firebombed on the news
on the TV
in the family room.

SOUNDTRACKS

Summers I lifeguard at the pool
blue like a canvas by Hockney.
Weekends I iron my hair
like Ali McGraw in *Love Story*,
dab Eau de Love or Love's Baby Soft
on my temples and between my breasts.

My California boy and me
in his father's Buick.
Above his heart, a scar I bless
with my mouth,
as hands reach through the radio
strumming us to divas in long white gloves,
singing *baby love oh baby love.*

I learn more
as I lie with my first love
in our first room,
his other scars,
on his knees and palms,
while Clapton sings
in a white room with black curtains
where shadows run from themselves.

I like to imagine it was like this
for mother and father—
making me in a cool room,
in a bed of heat.

BELLE DE JOUR

Dancing after school at Carole Bryan's house,
high on milk cartons in our white go-go boots
with zips up the back, we are Solid Gold Dancers
shaking and shimmying in fishnets and hot pants.

At slumber parties in our baby doll nighties,
nursing bottles of Coke, we watch *The Ed Sullivan*
Show—Mick doing his bump and grind in Ed's
censored version of "Let's Spend the Night Together."

We watch old movies, Deneuve,
as Severine, the bored housewife, batting
false eyelashes above a white push-up bra,
having sex with strangers,

and Eva Marie Saint, as Edie,
dropping her small white dress glove,
which Brando, as Terry, picks up
and pulls onto his brute boxer's paw.

At dawn, we strut through the house, Motown divas,
we perfect the gestures, hands cupping our hair,
up to our elbows in white evening gloves,
vamping to "Stop in the Name of Love."

LIBRETTO

They are shooting
Kennedy and King and Bobby.
Others are shooting
up, the boys on leave,
they're leaving
dog tags in the bars of Saigon
and the whore-houses of Hanoi—
their hobnail boots with the National Trust.

The National Guard are shooting
their own. Four dead in Ohio.

The KKK in their white robes
and masks are blowing
up four young girls
during Sunday service
at the Birmingham Sixteenth Street Baptist.

Motor City is burning
and Newark too exploding
under acetylene skies.

And the lynched are singing
we shall overcome.

And the The Beatles are singing
over a sitar.

And Simon and Garfunkel are singing
sounds of silence.

And soldiers in Nam are watching
water hyacinth float along the Mekong

Delta after the rains, humming in the jungle
an anthem by The Youngbloods

Darkness, darkness be my pillow
Take my head and let me sleep
In the coolness of your shadow
In the silence of your deep

We won't get fooled again.

ADAGIO

When father dies,
mother packs up the moon and stars.
She commits to the task of grief,
paces the half-dreamt rooms,
continues to punch the clock at the public library—
lost in books and sounds
of silence.

Outside in the garden of flowers
father named, spring's plaque of blooms,
maimed birches.
I clip rain-battered stalks
of white lilacs and iris,
I climb a tree like I did as a girl.
Perched in the weeping willow,
I dream of waking
in the wood of true stories.

Meanwhile, in the rubble
of the burned library in Sarajevo,
the cellist plays Albinoni's "Adagio in G Minor"
for twenty-two days, for twenty-two
killed waiting in a bread line.

The scroll of his cello
is a fist shaken in the face
of death.

DREAM OF BILLIE

In a bar hung with smoke, she smooths her
white satin dress over her hips, pulls
her evening gloves over
the curves of her elbows.
She runs her tongue along the bars
of "Strange Fruit."
Then she turns to me and says:
You can be in white satin, with gardenias
in your hair and no sugar cane for miles,
but you can still be working on a plantation.

High fever for days
the dream keeps me company.
Between worlds, I am plural—
I still hear Billie, her ravaged gravel
dream a little dream of me
over the steel of a streetcar
rattling my window.
In the white light of morning,
my eyes focus and notice
the fine hairs on your arms,
the whites of your eyes.
I realize you've held me
for hours, jazz cooling
the viral nights.

ELEGY

Now in our daughters' empty rooms,
the neural storms of their mother.
Our girls lie down with lovers,
each girl's face
my own.
I hear a trace
of their grandfather's lullabies
Soja, Raj kumari, soja—
Sleep, Princess, sleep.

On the stereo the Stones' "Paint It Black,"
U2's *Rattle and Hum,*
The Band's last waltz, "Helpless Helpless."

But I listen for strains
of father singing
along to Punjabi and Hindi ghazals

or Roger Whittaker
moi j'ai quitté mon pays bleu

as he slices oranges for me in morning
as I fold the turban he wears.
And I see him walking away
down the front lawn's
path like a part
in hair,
humming

I'm sad to say, I'm on my way
Won't be back for many a day...

AUGUST WEDDING: ANAND KARAJ

Deep calls to deep at the thunder of your cataracts:
all your waves and your billows have washed over me.

Psalm 42

Nothing is really lost. Take this white wedding
in the steepled church. After vows, stretch limos
slide down Saturday streets with cargoes of chiffoned
bridesmaids. At the reception, the bride and groom pray
for rosary miracles, drink the marriage wine,
release doves into the sky—covenants against broken hallelujahs.

Or take Veronese's "Wedding at Cana," the huge
canvas we saw in Paris—carnival courtyard
with its Doric and Corinthian columns,
musicians playing lutes and viola da gamba,
the dwarf holding a parrot—
Jesus and his mother haloed
under the butchered lamb,
guests with their goblets of wine and when
the wine runs out, Jesus turning the water into wine.

Years ago, restless before another wedding.
Our jeans slipped off,
my sari slung across your suited sleeve,
we enter my childhood home.
No bridal white or Indian red for me—
but a pale pink in between.

My aunties dress me, pleat lengths
of silk into my petticoat. I never learned
the art of the sari
and the heavy gold of Indian brides
weighs too much for me.

Father places the end of your *pulla* in my hand—
garments joined, you lead me, guided by father,
uncles, cousins, as if I might not find my way.

I am led by men in rings
around the book of scriptures,
the *Guru Granth Sahib*. Four times
around in the *Char Lavan*, ragas
sung with tabla and harmonium,
hymns and prayers in a mother tongue
foreign to me.

The relief on your Scottish
mother's face at the second ceremony
when we are double-ringed English.
The minister's voice *let us pray* in witness
and blessing and Holy Kiss and Amen.

Outside the church,
we are garlanded with flowers,
showered with petals.
At the reception,
I toss my clutch of orchids and roses,
ribbons streaming into my sister's
outstretched hands.

Years later, we're in the album—
I thought it was lost—
but there we are under vellum.
I dance with father to "All You Need Is Love."
On the next page, I've spun away
and across the floor to
the hook of your arm.

Nothing is really lost.
We pass the steepled church each day,
each of us separate, in and out of love
with the music of that long ago hour
when there is always a wedding, our own vows
sparking fire, when the wine is drained from the cup.

HUSH

All winter in stucco on 65th I learned to love
what couldn't speak: what began in milk and

blood. Baby, cat, the man who worked long weeks
away from home. Forty below.

Snow stiff trees burlapped against processions of
storms. I shovelled walks, nursed the baby, fed the cat.
Waited for the man I was slow to love.

Sometimes I'd ride the bus to the bistro,
only place in town that served espresso—
let it flow bitter down my throat—

the owners were Czech brothers in white shirts and black
trousers. They knew all about the baby, the cat, the man
I was slow to love.

At home, in silence, I folded laundry, changed diapers,
fed the cat, watched backyards fill with snow.

In spring, I woke, my mouth pressed to your back—
you—whom I was slow to love.

I never wrote about us, your arms around the baby,
around me, sealed into cracked plaster with a kiss.

WHAT BEGINS BITTERLY

Small talk in coffee shops.
An hour or a century clip-clops
by, fragile after argument.

Rain over the Hudson, your hair beaded with drops.
How the river accepts everything—bears away flyers
like flung bouquets. Along the walkway, joggers and dogs,
circus tent where trapeze artists fly and pitch
lessons to those who always wanted to fly.

Crepuscule sky bleeds orange, gilding the already
orange taxis gaudy. On an uptown street corner,
a woman wears small bones around her neck,
chatters to red-tailed hawks circling, lending
the skyscrapers living gargoyles or spreading wings
over Central Park where we traversed February ice
at the pace of monks, small talk flagging
by the Gates of Christo and Jeanne-Claude—
prayer flags the colour of Buddhist robes.

We were here once, years ago.
On the windshield, rain spitting.
On the radio, Marianne Faithfull spitting
"Broken English." Umbilical cord dragged across
burial grounds. Sheets of sex and cigarettes.
I, too, would dress in satin for absolution.
Midnight at the Chelsea Hotel.
We came for beauty,
tongues pierced with hallelujah.

Courtyard drift of jazz. In the music playing
every place we've been
every June too. Every moment you

were, to me, that one thing
shining. In the music playing
our living and our dying.
In this crowded room,
without moving a hand,
I touch you.

DRIVING HOME WITH CHET

Chet Baker on the stereo—
I imagine his Caravaggio face, heroin-
ruined in the single spot, as the horn comes
into languor, slow notes suffusing the groin—

applause for the trumpet's blue arrangements,
eighth notes slurring past slate roofs,
scattershots of sounds, familiar and strange—
cry of sirens, construction cranes—

kids playing at dusk, falling into their
own shadows on lawns like scissors—
metronomed scales of piano practice,
staccato of footsteps, coming home—

above the trumpet's metal and spit,
refrigerator hum, the din of phones,
someone coughs, someone hisses a white rage
for the song gone out of their bones—

ignition keyed quiet, Chet's last notes—
long vibrato shaping pain into order,
in the last crease of light—a wish,
thin as a knife.

STOP-TIME

At times I've travelled far from you—
brought to my knees by want
in white rooms in distant cities
and always, music phantoms me—
fevered, carnal—
the rock and roll of my youth,
the blues of Clapton and B.B. King,
the jazz dark and peeling,
Miles and Monk and Billie,
the straight statements of gospel,
Mahalia Jackson's every note a prayer
that reaches me for brief instants,
after dinner at Frederick's and Robert's
where gulls were circling,
seven settings of the sun sliding into English Bay.
I stood under the catalpa tree that sang white blossoms onto my hair
and through my fingers and I was home.
Blackbirds in the milk-blue light before dawn
scoring the silence.
Stop-time on the wet embouchure of a trumpet.
Music waiting in a white room,
white on white playing on
in the rabid world, and I your winter queen, your one and only.

GIVE US THIS DAY

our daily bread, we recited in unison, asking forgiveness
for our trespasses without knowing the meaning of trespass.
And lead us not into temptation, we chanted. *But deliver us from evil.*
For thine is the kingdom, and the power, and the glory,
for ever and ever. Over and over, led by teacher, our repetitions scoured
prayers into the earth's surface like wind, rain, thunder.
Day after day, yellow buses carried their charges
back to waiting mothers. Night after night, lovers kneeled
to each other as to no other. But now after
decades, a headline of Amish schoolgirls lined up against a chalkboard
for execution by bullet. We stand vigil for our ruined schoolyards.
And I start each day, kneeling to you as to no other. I lead
my classroom, and wash the black slate clean while they read.

DREAM OF A LITTLE BREAKFAST

In my dream my father brings me tea on a tray,
chota hazari in the early hours of morning,
like the servant in his boyhood—
tea poured in white china cups,
boiled milk under wrinkled skin.

I ask him to stay. I want to hear his voice.
Some canticle or ghazal or lullaby
or even “White Christmas.”
But I know this is not a hill station.
This is not his beloved Simla.
It is winter in Ontario, the only sound

a footfall crunch across frosted fields.

AIN'T NO CURE

I slice oranges in the kitchen.
The countertop worn, notched
with the story of the knife.

I've been reading Ovid's *Cure for Love.*
You circle my waist with your arms—
kiss the back of my neck.
I remember who we were—
the taste of us sweet and dangerous,
the girl and boy on the front porch
cooling our heels on our way
to the grave.

We believed we could make something
in the dark.

METROPOLIS

2005

MEMORY PALACE

The air above the city is saturated
with prayers. Like the air in
industrial towns and dreams,
it's hard to breathe.

Below, an aerial view of the apartment
where we used to make love. Nightmare
demolition site, cement rubble, explosion
of mortar and brick, gargoyle beheaded.

In memory—
the unfastened blouse,
your hands stroking my hair.
The world seen through a child's snow globe.

In the yard we make snow angels
rising from where we've lain on our backs,
flying like children, leaving imprints of
wings and gowns.

Like Cicero's memory palace,
assigned with beauty or ugliness,
dressed up with cloaks or crowns,
disfigured by stains of blood or mud or paint,

there is a love which cannot be moved.
It must die in its place and in its time,
destroyed together with the building
in which it stands.

And in this way, we will remember.

THE NEW REPUBLIC OF LETTERS

If I speak for the corpses I hold in my hand,
I must praise the madness that put them there,
speak in a human music,
a language that awakens us in
a Republic of Prayer.

Here, there are magicians finding
coins behind our ears,
chalk between my fingers,
graffiti blackboards,
your hands cupping my breasts.

I have saved your kisses
behind my knees,
in the hollow of my clavicle,
a suitcase full of your poems from the time
before your descent, the Gauloise smell of
your stranger's coat.

Here, the poet is voice,
memory of the guillotine,
sounds of erasure and delight.
Kiss my throat until my
belly tightens. Give me a recitative,
vowels engraved upon my scars,
light written on the roof of my mouth.
Rub my feet with milk.

Requiem of plain speech.
I write towards your mouth.
Your language sets my hands on fire.

When you can no longer cheat death,
I will close your eyes as I promised,
for need has been our covenant,
our common salt at the end of mercy.

I will close your eyes as I promised.
Then I will eat your heart.

SEEING

Oh my city, emerald
buried in ravines, coyotes
prowl your meridians.

I am writing from the road.
I had to see clearly
the single world.

I could describe to you
the lemon groves, the beggared streets,
palaces of gold and marble,
all the cities I travelled
to sit in cafés,
to feel the underworld of subways,
to see vanquished cities burned,
men and woman cradling the slain,
jilted sweethearts in every theatre,
to know—there is no consolation except in desire,
only the occasional small bird singing,
a temporary clearing of the disorder of things,
that flushes the throats of politicians and warriors,
pours a river of poetry through the larynx.

In the city of the future
the world is bandaging its limbs
against wholesale murder,
bombed schoolyards.
From the crazed skulls of high-rises,
needle towers on love's black sea,
the wind overturns someone's sail.
The city is a glass book.
Open it with an unflinching hand of
a severed arm. Read the pages
to the lilt of a nightingale.

The sights and fires of
your streets are cleaved
to me. You stand immutable.
Beauty is in the coming home.

What is ordinary is not possible anymore.

Your towers rise in me.
A different wind turns the vane.
What I am waiting for
is just now being born.

TESTAMENT

In a city ruled by pigeons and doves, I see citizens moving mysteriously in the streets as if in a silent movie. I want to speak out to them but the world is deafened by the cries of birds, by the flap of wings. I imagine voices that taste of colours and flavours. I imagine describing these sounds to the deaf, a voice like vanilla, or orange, or a voice that smells like brandy. I count the birds in the square at City Hall as if some numerical sequence would be a code to explain the digits I have memorized: the phone numbers of the dead. Sometimes I dial those numbers, profess my love to anyone who picks up the receiver. Catalogue of memories in my hands, thickening in spiral notebooks. The city offers me a biography of rain, every vowel beating against its granite heart.

METROPOLIS REDUX

1

The city sometimes forgets where she lives. The streets are confused. Air of cinders and flowers, the nerves of the boulevards on edge. Parks desert themselves. The address of her future uncertain.

She grabs for the world, tenants a coach house among restored Victorians, rose gardens and fountains. Brick walls dream of hay and horses, the scent of leather harnesses, ghosts tangled in their tethers. The soiled gloves of the coachman, carriage of sleep. A lost earring, a midnight slipper.

Outside her bedroom, graffiti across the road reads:

Tom Hendry is a rat

Testified against his older brother for murder

Full moon pinned between skyscrapers, the alley becomes a night-river of smashed beer bottles, obscenities screamed by crack dealers and drunks.

2

In the empty theatres of the city, small productions are played out. Rain-slicked streets. Stories of charred roses, bones of mishap. A star plummets and a soul is exiled. In the storm of dreams, the cup of sleep. A doorway haunted by an open hand, ambulance wail, the coroner's arms.

We are made of nothing that contents us.

Any backward glance is fictive.

3

She wants hands for making violins—but for the rest of her life she searches for words that will not come. Amnesia becomes an approach to understanding her life.

She closes the locket, presses parted lovers face to face. Rubs her own image in the mirror until she disappears.

4

Humid summer and she remembers love in the fever of other cities—New Orleans French Quarter rot and filigree, fungal tropic, white cups of chicory at Café du Monde.

Paris hauntings of Saint-Sulpice, Delacroix angels, camellias and blown roses. Lovers in the Jardin du Luxembourg. Ruined gardens weep. The scent of Billie Holiday's gardenias. In Montparnasse cemetery, Brancusi's stone kiss, "Le Baiser."

Night smell of lilies. A woman wakes. Releases luna moths among the stars. Love is mistaken sometimes. The hardness of pity bleeds her to the bone.

5

Power blackout. The bride unveiled discovers the bridegroom is a leaky vessel in a blasted marriage.

She tells her lover, you have come too close.

In the panic streets, she is determined to live life with her hair flying back like the tail of a race horse.

She does not want love letters. They have no medicinal value. Intimacy is shameful unless it is perfect.

Even in a lover's arms, the language of lack. Loneliness is the truth of things.

6

Citizens work the armatures, bitter locks of anger. She tells her lover, I see all the cities in you and me. Our bodies coated with silver, feet chafed by pavements of foreign towns.

Transparent city. Vigil in mortal air. Vodka in the icebox. Our words like incisions balanced on a bloodaxe. Mother's keepsakes: child's lock of hair, milk teeth, hospital bracelets.

Morning cool as pearls. Her lover tucks something inside her, labial secret *memento mori*   decree of one perfect thorn.

7

The metropolis waits, protects itself from Kafka's prophecy in *Arms of the City*. The senselessness of the heaven-reaching tower. No absoluteness. The city could be destroyed by five successive blows from a gigantic fist.

The wind is collapsing the ribs of the chapels, every altar-stone skewed. In the path of resistance, the city doors are locked down. We ride the train to the edge, where the buildings meet the mouth of the harbour. The boxcars slice a path, leave a stiff suture. We hope the train will ease into Union Station, deliver a state of grace, some sacred ground, where all things lost are recovered.

8

In gunfire streets children are burned instead of fuel. She recites their names. Children of Sharpeville, Sarajevo, Kigali, Beslan—infinite list of cities.

Something turned loose in a child's sorrow. November with graves. Infancy white turns to roan and black. Her words hold the scent of madness as her daughter disappears into a woman. Eyes peer through the windows of ruined houses. Visions of apothecary glass, christening gowns in armoires.

Necropolis. Burnt sorrow in tank-rutted fields. Gangrenous stench. Bed soaked in music.

Scorched, we are cherrying the brain.
Gothaming the mind.

At the city's edge   cooling towers.

9

Dirigibles hover in the city's spires. Tattoo artists ink waiting limbs. The woman waits on the platform.

This place is not where she began. But here, her body has spilled blood and water, emptying towards the future. Fresh scars are ordained. The city gives her voice, something singular chosen out of chaos.

Memory repeats itself so that the city can exist. Spring batters the mock orange into blossom. Even the trees hunger for music. Someone throws stones on the roof. She practises arpeggios among the bodies in bloody rags, the streets full of cries.

10

The armadas are unleashed into cities and harbours. In the sudden suck of air, she sleeps the sleep of apples. When the city grows down into her eyes, it steals away her infant sight. All history in centuries of bodies, floating in canals, blooming in houses and streets, all flesh hungering, loving, relinquishing, aging, spending itself, the world moving through the corridor of the body, resting sometimes at the vulnerable places, the temples.

Tenderness is our best gesture in the face of death.

11

She notices light in the elms. In night kitchens and apartment bedrooms. In the park—the junkie's delicate fingers, newly hatched birds.

And in the rose heat of the lung—the poem that will not hold its tongue—refuses to shut its scarlet mouth.

STILL LIFE

Saturday morning. You gift me with
the newspaper in bed.
I read of the capital city of Slovenia
called *Ljubljana,* meaning Beloved.
There they claim poetry as a national disease.
A province of tenderness where they
too have known the thorn of love.

And here you are—your shoulder
propping up the ruined world.
Under the covers, our bodies practise
living as if our city was on fire.
My hands cover you with poems
that assume another life
unbroken.

In our bed ribboned with newsprint
the world is still with longing.
We put it to our lips and drink.
Your heart in my skull.

DREAM SEQUENCE WHEN THE MOON IS RAINING

In the end we don't know what we want
until we are ghosts already

these days
when you have let loose your words into the lethal air
your mouth full of failed prayer
you will remember the adulterous heart
                anonymous hotel rooms
take the wrapper off the bathroom glass
                bend your head to drink
                feel the knuckle of solitude

you will smell the stench of several centuries
screaming testimony
as you build a tiger life
                hear the noise of your blood
the fevered heart burns
even the grass grieves

the palsied hand will wrench everything back from its pit of darkness
what is ruined, broken off will be restored to you

you will hear the girl in the next apartment
playing Elgar on a rented cello

renunciation so hard to learn
                becomes ecstasy in the
melancholy music of bone

you will feel affection's gift
the world abundant in harsh light
elsewhere, someone buried up to her armpits
is being stoned to death

elsewhere, the witness tree reaches for us
elsewhere, the same story repeats itself

we are lost in winter's ache
                    this cankered season
undoing the self a hard road alongside tenderness

What can I offer my heart up to?

small armageddons
in the waters of disremembering
I will lay me down

mercy made of fire
the century burning in the world's noise
I dream of my left side opened
                    my heart removed

la luna piove how the moon rains into
our dreams of gold *sogni d'oro*
starvelings feed from my mouth

in the moments when you ask to be taken
my hand that has passaged you
will open veins of tenderness
my mouth will suck out your demons

on the days when it is all too much to bear
remember the music that leaves you undone
and every lover's name.

PSALM

In the city where I live
A man is arrested for abducting and
Butchering a twelve-year-old girl.

Tonight it rains and I walk
On streets that reek
Of rust and pitch.

Petitions to any god are uncertain.
The sky is spread with vast wings of lead.
No oracular assurance from the pulpits.

Still I pray
Words coming like blood on the mouth.
That the sweet taste be taken from the violent thought
That in the birdless hours
The mother and father of the twelve-year-old girl
Will be granted dreamless sleep
That the lachrymal salt of this rain
Will become original milk.

FILM NOIR

At the Gare Centrale
She fingers the blue
Of her Canadian passport.

Wears the shoes she bought
From the *marché aux puces.*

Crimson, strapped at her ankles
They once belonged to a dancer
At the Moulin Rouge.

At each city limit
A border to be crossed.
Every language a new currency.

At the hotel
She befriends the night porter.
Tells him secrets
Intimate stories of her life.

She is conscious of the weight
Of inheritance.
The heft of her mother's rubies
Sewn into the hem
Of her skirt.

Insured
She knows there is always
Someone willing to bargain for the past.

CITY OF MADNESS AND LOVE

What then of madness,
    of putting things badly,
    of our fallibility?
Do we believe we'll do better next time?

What then of love,
    in the alleyways of the city,
    in the smoke fume of drink.
Someone is always having a hard time of it, right?

What then of desire,
    of endless appetite, carnal urgency,
    tasting it everywhere,
when according to philosophy, life is suffering, death a promised land.

What then of the insomniac,
    each night exchanged for something
    darker than imagined?
Someone stunned by the power of his rage.

What then of reading Schopenhauer,
    of the dissatisfied, egotistical state,
    of words fit for the newborn.
Is the city more than will and representation?

What then of her,
    sunlit scars on her forearm,
    believing there is something euphonious
in doves crying for the inconsolable.

READING LIKE A GIRL

2004

LET ME TELL YOU OF THE SACRED

She is there in my dreams
the child made of our holiest hours.

The child you and I will never have.

If the sacred could speak for itself
it would be whispered through her
in the way we would wake her
                                        in her halo of dark curls

in her hand outstretched to yours.

GATHERING LILACS

Every street is a confluence
of dreams, of lips to stars.
Everywhere I travel there is still this—
a small girl in her red dress.
Her father clasps her hand in his, teaches her
the convulsive beauty of things
as they walk through the garden
gathering flowers.

All her days she wanders
the sacred, the strange, through lost altars.
All her days she longs for the thing
that would fill her life.

In the heat-stoned afternoon
the air is drenched with the scent of lilacs.
I cut bunches loose with kitchen shears,
quench them
in every available vase and bowl, arrange
them on sills, and mantels and ledges.

At midnight I gather armfuls for you,
place them on the bed, tuck them between
sheets, lay them against the rough of your
cheek, against the veins of your sleeping eyelids
as I finish your dreams.

These days every street leads me
to you, where love is negligent,
laying bare everything,
recognition rustling in leaves.

PRIMER

The girl reads neighbourhoods of
dog, cat, sister, brother, mother, father,
houses lit with yellow sunshine and once
upon a time glass slippers
and long-toothed wolves.

* * *

The girl does not know yet
                                        the broken world,
that there will be pages for *consequence, coercion, fraudulence.*

Outside her room
the sky is an X-ray pinned to light
                              armies of birds lifting into skeletal shadows.
Softness vanishes in the city
                              deformed by *contagion, fear, vanity.*

News stories convulse
                              palsied in the laws of speech.
Planes pass over the skyline.
Traffic lights change voltage.
Damage is quiet

                              oil slick pools in city parkades
fissured winds, smudge of newsprint.
Elegant hands read the book of lost entries
          trace the red glares of exit signs, writing on tenement walls
                                                            the veined arms of junkies.

* * *

The girl reads her picture books.
A child's garden of verses.
The alphabet sifts into her ribcage
opens her to stars, grass, abcs
whole sentences whispering dark.

In the open doorway
something cold and distant
even adult hands are small against it.

The book left on the lectern
brittle yellow pages without context
lexicons of disclosure
soft imprisonment.

The girl does not know yet how words will
hiss
tremble on fuller pages—
an imagined wilderness
an insomniac's tale
seductions
remembrances—
forgettings—
a wrecked lullaby—
a deep song of mouth
unnaming the known.

* * *

My hands close on empty testimonies
until I find that girl—a pocket of held light
ripped corner of an illuminated manuscript.

In my dreams I see her
the pages blowing with dormant
                                        terror
as she gathers moon and sky
in her small hands like a mouth-lovely language
that has no word for *harm*.

READING LIKE A GIRL: 2

The comic-book heroes I loved best
were the mutants and freaks.
Spiderman, Batman, and Aquaman who was half-fish.

And then there was Wonder Woman. She was glorious,
descended from the Amazons of Greek myth. She had
fabulous breasts, a tiara, a magic lasso and belt, red boots,

and bulletproof wristbands to remind her of the folly
of submitting to men's domination. If a man could bind
an Amazon's wrists, she lost her powers.

In early stories she captures spies—
Third World War promoters—
sends them to imprisonment on Venus,

where they are forced to wear Girdles of Magnetic Gold
to tame them into peaceful life. She defeats the evil Fausta,
Nazi Wonder Woman in "Wanted by Hitler, Dead or Alive."

Wonder Woman was beautiful and powerful as a hero,
understated and reserved in her secret identity as Diana Prince,
the secretary in her smart-chick glasses.

She taught me radical truth.
The geek, the hybrid mutant is a treasure,
so easily misunderstood in real life

a secret identity is necessary. Hold it close.
Protect your wrists.
Put on your red boots. Step into fire.

READING LIKE A GIRL: 3

Reading my mother's magazines,
Ladies' Home Journal and *Miss Chatelaine,*
pictures of women with cinch-waist dresses,
bouffant hairdos. They ride in convertibles
headscarves keeping every hair in place.

These women are so happy with their pink and aqua
kitchen appliances. In one ad for Scott toilet paper,
the woman wears an evening gown in the exact
pastel blue of the toilet paper and Kleenex tissue.

These women use Yardley Lavender and Cashmere Bouquet
talcum powder. They buy new davenports and credenzas. Pictured
in exotic landscapes in their underwear, they dream in their Maidenform
bras and girdles that promise to set them free.

The ad I like best is for the black lace corset called a Merry Widow.
Under the sedate hairdo and perfect makeup of the model,
her Max Factor red lips whisper
It's simply wicked what it does for you.
Care to be daring, darling?

READING LIKE A GIRL: 4

At our school, girls are separated from boys,
gathered in the school gymnasium.
The nurse distributes pamphlets about
life cycles and Kotex. Glossy brochures,
pristine and sanitized, with the beautiful fresh-faced
girl, blonde hair swept back with pink
satin ribbon. We read all about this girl and
know we will soon become her, young women
leading Breck girl lives.
We learn our lessons well, believe we can
hold on to our well-groomed dreams.
It takes us years before we realize how many
things will make us bleed, how easy
for the world to rip us to pieces.

READING LIKE A GIRL: 5

Long after my mother thought I was asleep,
late into the night, I would read under the
covers with a flashlight. How I loved them,

the stories about the girl detectives,
reading and recording the world in notebooks—
the ones who solved crimes with their

wits, their brains, their All-American good looks.
I drove that blue roadster with Nancy Drew,
dated Ned, looked lovely and charming

and desirable at college football games.
And how I dreamed of being Cherry Ames, student
nurse, with her stylish cap and uniform, her black

hair and rosy cheeks, her boyfriend and adventures.
And when I grew up, I became them, Nancy and Cherry.
I cut off my long black braids, styled my hair into a bob.

I became the girl detective, the nurse, capable of building
nations and soothing the hearts of men—
for a while.

READING LIKE A GIRL: 6

The volume of Tolstoy thumbs her open.
She tries to keep the heroine alive.

Outside the library windows
ragged moths beat against the streetlamps.
She feels the heat of locomotive steam
rising from the stacks, weeps when she
sees Anna's red purse on the tracks.

She closes the book with stunned hands
as if she had touched the hem of a final
morning, a sense of that going into it alone.
She begins to think she will not be carried
unscarred, untorn into any heaven. Wants
someone to hold her while she burns.

SLOW DANCING: BEACONSFIELD 1973

Parents away for the weekend
we are in a house like all the others,
freshly painted trim and gabled windows,
brass-numbered door and neatly pruned hedges,

and the basement recreation room is overflowing
with us, sweet sixteens, bodies clutched together in sweat in
the cigarette smoke and beer, slow dancing to Chicago's "Color
My World" and Led Zeppelin's "Stairway to Heaven."

My girlfriends and I wear angora sweaters our mothers
bought for us in the soft pastel shades of infants: fingernail
pink, baby blue, pale yellow, and cream. We wear drugstore
scents named for innocence and fruit: Love's Baby Soft, Love's Fresh
Lemon—or the more sophisticated Eau de Love or Revlon's Charlie.

For years, we have danced in ballet studios, spinning, dreaming
our mothers' dreams of Sugar Plum Fairies,
our rose tight confections, pink slippers twirling
pas de deux jetés, pirouetting our taut muscles until our toes bled.

But tonight, we dance in our tight blue Levi's, our mothers' voices
fading as Eric Clapton's electric guitar shivers our spines, the music
claiming us, and we spill out under the streetlamps, dancing across
equators into the earth's light.

On the streets of suburbia, this is the beginning of hunger.
It catches me by surprise, exploding like a kiss.

SOMEWHERE, A WOMAN IS WRITING A POEM

Somewhere, a woman is writing a poem
as she tucks her child into bed,
bends over her desk in the yellow lamplight and frees her hand
to write, breaking through the page like that Dorothea Tanning

painting where the artist's hand gashes through the canvas,
fingers and wrist plunged to the bone.
She writes a dark, erotic psalm, an elegy,
a poem to grow old in, a poem to die in.

Somewhere, a woman is writing a poem
as she gives away the clothes of her dead loved ones,
as her words rise in her mind, rosaries of prayer for the dying children,
for the ones who have disappeared: the *desaparecido*.

Somewhere, a woman is writing through the taste
of fear and rage and fury. She writes in milk and blood.
Somewhere, a woman who thought she could say nothing
is writing a poem.

THEOLOGY

This is always what it comes to.

The decision to understand *significance.*

How love's meaning is held in that moment
full of terror, rage, grief, tenderness, trust,

that round, full moment undeniable
like the mouth closed on the sweetness of an orange

like the flesh kissed again and again in the warm falling rain.

This is it—held out to you for the taking.

Accidental. Raw as faith.

ALPHABET

Angel he calls me, *angel* says the
Boy on the street when I give him a dollar.
Choreography everywhere in the city,
Crows wheeling and dancing on the horizon, every cell recalls
Desire, Billie Holiday's *distingué* lovers, slick, slippery memories of
Evenings drunk with stars and rain and
Frank Sinatra crooning love letters like
Grace notes in the summer air.
Heat hisses on the boulevards,
Inches over our skins like imagined sighs and opium smoke,
Jack Kerouac screams out, *angel!* on a midnight moving train.
Kisses for the junkies eating oranges.
Love a one-word intangible cipher.
Many-mouthed birds sing *Kyrie Eleison*
Nocturnes and nightingales singing in the city
Open wide the hearts of the innocent and the not-so-innocent.
Pink the colour of Ginger Rogers' shoes turned pink
                    with blood
                    after Fred asks for hundreds of takes for a single scene.
Queens and transvestite divas dance in the street in a costume parade.
Ruined beauty—we can always be romantic and pray for its return.
Stubbornness is underrated. It spines us,
Threading us through the lives of those we barely know
Until each of us becomes the ash and bone of the other.
Vanity tricks us until the collapse on bloody feet
When hobo skies dream us into adventures of comic-book heroes with
X-ray vision, new gods of the city
Yawping across skycrapers and apartment buildings,
Zest of their goodness like an absolute, tasted on the wind.

SOJA

In my parents' bedroom
the bureau holds the gifts he gave her,
lingerie drawers of lace and silk, peignoir sets of filmy chiffon,
bottles of perfume Chanel No.5, Miss Dior, Je Reviens.

Silver-framed photographs on the nightstand,
lives stilled in sepia and Kodachrome.
There we are, the three of us on Parliament Hill among
tulips, my mother in her red sari, red shoes, red handbag,
my father with his turban, me in my British duffle coat with
the pointed hood, blue like the one Paddington Bear wore.

Another snapshot.
My father teaching me to skate on Rideau Canal,
to lie in fresh powder and make snow angels.

In this one I am walking with my mother
in the Gatineau Hills in the flame of maple trees,
dressed to match our new country,
my mother in her orange printed sari,
me in my orange frock sashed at my waist.

A hand-tinted photo. My mother in her '50s bathing suit,
posing in front of the rounded curves of our blue Ford.
Coke bottles cooling in the sand, lined up along the shoreline.

There is my mother in her sari in front of Niagara Falls.
In another shot the three of us are standing under the falls
in our shiny yellow slickers.

I know the gleam and smell of the polished
leather of his shoes, buffed every morning
before he left for work.

I press my face into the crisp white cotton of his shirts,
brush my cheek against his jackets, sweaters still warm with him.
I touch my teeth to the metal of his watch, his cufflinks.

I can hear his voice reading fairy tales, singing
Harry Belafonte's "Jamaica Farewell"
My heart is down, my head is turning around
I had to leave a little girl in Kingston town

I hear him singing Punjabi and Hindi ghazals, lullabies

Soja Raj kumari, soja,
Soja meethe sapne aayan
Soja pyari Raj kumari

Sleep, princess, sleep
Sleep with sweet dreams
Sleep beloved princess

In the hush, I am cradled by the sound of him,
voice lifting me like birdsong through the pyre.

In my mother's house I enter silence,
wear it as a dress, my father's ashes acrid
in my throat, I remember the days of savage
adoration, child for father, father for child, when
I was tiny enough to stick to his trousers like a burr.
His sudden vanishing a brute sledgehammer blow.

FIRST LESSONS: POST-COLONIAL

Every morning my mother would
part my hair down the middle, plait
it into long braids reaching down to
my waist. I would walk with the other
neighbourhood kids to Briarwood Elementary
School, absent-minded, face always
in a book, reading as I walked, dressed like
the other girls in navy tunics, white blouses,
novitiate-like collars.

Those days, my knees were always scraped
and skinned from roller-skating on the concrete
slopes of Avondale Road, my skate keys around
my neck, flying, weightless—
my father continuously swabbing my cuts with
hydrogen peroxide, scabs peeking out over the
tops of white kneesocks and my Oxford shoes.

In class, we stood at attention,
spines stiffened to the strains of singing
"God Save the Queen" to the Union Jack,
recited The Lord's Prayer
hallowed be thy name, learned lessons
from Gideon's Bible.

In geography and history the
teacher would unroll the giant map of
the world from the ceiling, use her
wooden pointer to show the countries
of the Empire, the slow spread of a faded
red stain that marked them soft burgundy
like the colour of my father's turbans.

Ancient history. Crisp whites of cricket
matches at officers' clubs. Afternoon tea
in the pavilion.

Decades later I can reconstruct the
story, move past the pink glow.
If that surface was scratched
the pointer would fly along the contours of
the parchment world, across the Himalayas,
through emerald coils of steaming rivers.
Under my fingernails, the scents of spices
and teas, the silk phrasings of my mother's
saris, the stench of imperial legacy, blood
spilled from swords on proper khaki uniforms
lanced through the bodies of Sikh soliders at
the front lines of her Majesty's British Army.
But our teacher never said, *Remember this.*

READING CHEKHOV

Reading Chekhov. Stories about love,
  the sadness of his characters, always meeting each other too late.
Missed lives, mourning what could have been,
                    departing forever in railway stations.
Tears, a lorgnette raised to the eye, ice etched on windows,
          gaslit winter scenes
                    a loveless marriage in a country house in a town
                    like all the others.

I'll read the story differently. A Chekhov love letter.

Love me through departures,
through the faltering valves of your heart,
                    the ticking of clocks and moving trains.

Kiss me in the cleft of each elbow, behind each knee.

* * *

Buddhists tell us to live our days unattached
                                        to the dust of the world
                                          to enter the blackness.
To always see ourselves as light.

Not so easy to do when the hum of the world
                                              dulls us in its gears.
I am trying to wear light as a garment,
                    to find it in the paradise of afterlife under a stone
                    in the opened door of a commuter train.

Departure lounge at the airport.
Goodbye a salt-water word you avoid
                    as if it would open a wound that would never close.

Goodbye a word of red waves, fog-horn sobs, sea-wracked,
tongue-uttered ache,
ember of pain in the wrist, a movement towards
the corrosive heart.
Goodbye a word that makes your bones scream a word you dare not breathe.

* * *

I am always naked with you.
The winds brought me newborn into your arms
to the one who holds me through the night.

I have always known you.
My harsh blessing.
Every sweetness has the taste of your skin.
Each wound has the shape of your mouth.

Forget me. As I would forget you. For the suffering.

Remember me. As I would remember you. Claim the way the heart stops when you come to me naked and scratched.
Climb to my bed bleeding
on the dark wind of dreams.

* * *

I have waited for you all my life.
Four decades to find you
and still and still a story that turns back on itself.

Dance with me, beloved.
I am your wild, sweet girl.
I would have you as you are,
aging and heartsick with the world.

*   *   *

All night, all night you can have this book.
Turn the pages on your lap, until they become like well-worn linen,
last words soft in your hands.

Meet me there in that story.

LECTOR IN FABULA

I am reading in a school of dreams,
a lost girl in a night's tale, wandering through
a *jardin d'essais*, underfoot, the crunch of pale
green lichen on the forest floor.

Hyacinth gardens fade into a scene of city lights and
I am on Vancouver's Hastings Street.
The pages become stained with East End rot, humanity
pumping heroin through collapsed veins and there

on the corner is a woman weeping, the sound of
her pain palpable in every crack of concrete,
a prostitute whose knees have been broken by
a man with a baseball bat.

I take her by the hand and dream her home with me,
wash her body and her crushed limbs,
her sore-covered feet. I try to absorb her fever
in my touch, lay her down to sleep in my bed.

In the morning when I wake, she is gone,
only a cool, clear light shining on the tumbled sheets.

Tonight, I'll turn the pages of the book again,
my hands inside the spine, reading the places
where memory doesn't work.

READING AMY LOWELL

Summer and I have returned to the town where
                                        I was a young wife,
where we raised our daughters.
The name of the place means *a place to live forever.*
Mythology and daily life. Legends of sea serpents,
ghosts of horses lost swimming in from the island, tangled with
slow-pitch tournaments, ballplayers and Winnebago campers,
tourists on the beaches and lunching at wineries.

Today I am marking freshman English papers in the backyard.
The air is sweet and fugitive. In the gardens, wild strews of roses,
pink blooms amidst the silver foliage of planted pathways,
                    fragrance spilling from their thorn beds,
the morning stillness stung by the
screeching of Steller's jays and flocks of crows
                              singing a crude chorale.

In the distance, the sound of ducks landing on the swimming pool,
                              splashing and flapping their wings.
My daughters laugh and I am struck by that particular radiance
              again and again   how the laughter of girls
                            cuts through blue air.
How did I come to this place,
                    the professor circling sentence fragments,
the occasional leap of the heart when a student writes a beautiful phrase.
My student has written an essay on Amy Lowell.
And suddenly I am transported, back to 1972 at Beaconsfield High
in Mr. Whitman's North American Literature class,
                                        yes that was his name.

Fifteen years old, sitting in those straight-backed wooden chairs,
my legs cramped under the tiny desk with my huge Norton anthology
open at Amy Lowell's "Patterns."
There have been so many poems I have committed to heart.
This poem was one of them.
I could taste this poetry, feel the rhythms of it beating in my eyelids.
For the first time, reading Amy Lowell,
I understood that burnt cadence of sense,
the quickstep of syllables in my throat.

I wrote an essay on Amy Lowell's "Patterns,"
something about the Imagist movement, the poet's use of figurative
language and form
in a consideration of how societal expectations may
inhibit a woman's actions in society.

Mr. Whitman gave me an A on my essay.

I promptly forgot what I knew about patterns
in the wisdom of my sixteenth year.

I must have known then, something about the effect of patterns,
knowing Lowell's narrator, the feel of her corset, her pink and silver
brocade gown, how she grieves for her dead lover,
how a heavy-booted lover would have loosened
the stays of her stiff correct brocade
in the pink and silver garden,
the bruise and swoon of it.

I too am a rare
Pattern.

In dreams I see the husband of my girlhood,
my pink and silver time,
his arms around me like a familiar blanket.

He is holding something out to me, places it in my palm—
                        a scroll, a tablet, some lost history inscribed,
                                                        unreadable.

And centuries pass and we are still *gorgeously arrayed*
                                              trousseaus pink and silver,
mouths stuffed with bone china
pink and silver, boned and stayed

Christ! What are patterns for?

At sixteen I used to mouth the words,
                                        swords springing from the repetitions,
from the ribs of consonants.

Today, I reread the poem and the body flies apart,
remembering how a grown woman can brush back her hair in moonlight,
watch her husband and daughters inside her house as if in a dream.

Remembering days when the woman wakes up and she understands her skin
doesn't fit her anymore.

What she does inside that skin leaves
                          her outside her house in long nights of crickets
                                        singing and the lake whispering.

Sometimes, she longs to be like characters in a novel or a poem,
                                        the relief of flatness on paper.

The heart is literate.
                        It wants to read the pages it has unfurled.
It wants the grip of roses on love-ridden afternoons,

                        the ordinary TV, chair, table, plate, sneakers
entangled through a sky of blood tracery swept innocent by rain.

I want conversation that is like the stripped truth of the poem,
the way I felt when I first read Amy Lowell's "Patterns."
Over the years I wondered what kind of shelter
I could make with words.
I search for the colour of home in the extravagance of reading.
I am looking for it still.

This town is not a place for introspection. Such beauty.
The lake, the blue air, the sun, all defy me
to find some fault in this horizon.

Over the years I weaned my babies, got ready to walk
into the pink and silver light.

BENEDICTION

Because hands afraid of loss are the only hands for love.
—Yehuda Amichai

Wittgenstein writes that when the eye beholds beauty,
the hand wants to paint it.

I want to commit you to ink,
indigo blue scrolled with blood.

In the cradle of your hands,
lies the grave of my mouth.

Your hands rebuild me,
hammer together the hinges of my ruined bones.

Your hands make flowers of things.
Many forms of tenderness bloom in your palms.

Your hands wrench open the history I bear.
My black vault is unlatched for you to enter.

Let me begin every day like this, in these first hours,
grief lifted in your dawn-soaked hands.

AMAS VERITAS

Fear is always your first word.
You hear it in the wind.
The weight of love grows soft with despair.

Your ghosts are between us.
You will die from the false song
                    in the full sentence of the fugue.
Bury ghosts in the woods,
                    dig their graves at the crossroads.

The moon will deliver us from evil
                                    or from love.

* * *

We survive until morning.
Sleep covers your face soaked with light.
In the room's heavy scent I watch your breathing.

Remember the warm suspended darkness,
                                        cool dusks,
your flesh made sweet by the thick-walled
chambers of your mother's heart.

I am with you at your moment of waking,
lodged between tooth and tongue.

We do not choose to love.
It breaks us and we obey.

SACCADE

The chronicle of the city unravels
like a prayer cloth
calm of storybook nurseries, book codes
swift calligraphy of desire.

The city dreams us
gives us exigencies in eavesdropped
stories, undistinguished pleadings
requiems for forgetting.

There is a small star pinned where Hiroshima used to be.

It's late and someone's almost forgotten how to convince you
he's telling the truth.
Even in sleep he cries out for help
and you minister to him
a woman like history returning for its wounded.

Blackbirds drop from telephone wires
rose petals collect in birdbaths.

* * *

Everything stories you. You take Rilke at his word
Taste it everywhere. Wonderland signs
Eat me. Drink me.

Your hands, like hobbled birds,
read the classics. The hero enters the arched gate of the city.
In these books it is clear where the story of the city begins.
In the book of lost entries
nothing is pure but the forgotten things

crossed out words on a haunted page
useless dark of ink.

* * *

Today the city is unwriting itself
in a coffin of glass.

In the blurred doorways
in skyscrapers that rise silver and blue
cool as if nothing could ever make them burn.

Sprayed on concrete walls
Where is my beautiful daughter
Emma was here
Escúchame
I'll pray for you Lucas
Fuck the politicians
Recuérdame
Inamorata

the billboard with the women tall
with long legs against white sand and blue ocean
red mouths puckered high above the crowds
smooth lipsticked smiles longing for cigarettes and sex.

Across the city, lights are shutting off
Good night, good night.

On the radio, the sirens are singing
Emmylou Harris, Alison Krauss, Gillian Welch
ethereal lullaby *Didn't Leave Nobody But the Baby*

Come lay your bones
on the alabaster stones
and be my ever-lovin' baby

Reading Emily Dickinson
Beauty crowds me till I die.
You feel the loneliness.
That's what is left of the dream of beauty.

Beauty
so many kinds to name.

You hope for a day soft at the edges
for something, someone to
know the small hands of rain
to be like rain
wet with a decent happiness.

* * *

Kiss the gleaming armour of the world.
Feel its electric purr.
Close your hands on wind-stunned leaves.
Buff the scars of history with your mouth.

RETABLOS

For the prayerbook,
someone to thumb it open every day.

For the woman whose mind paces in fever in its bone cage,
a circuitry of prayers, hymnals as salve.

For the insomniac,
a lullaby that sings like the nod of heroin.

For the girl with braces on her teeth, a smile of her own,
a grin the size of this room.

For the one who is frightened by the power of his own rage,
a night without the thickness of terror.

For the ones whose ribcages have fallen, ashes rising to meet dust,
the arms of the world for a little while.

For the girl in Tijuana who asked for a dollar in exchange for taking
her photograph, a fat bank account.

For the imprisoned Cuban poet who was tortured, made to eat her own
words, her books in every bookstore, library, and school of the world.

Nothing is lost unless we make it so.

For the one who has chosen to make it so,
my kiss upon your torn wings, the thorn of your heart.

CLAIM

All she did was read. This left a commotion in her wake. Reading as faith. Book as talisman.

Startled breath. Childhood sets of golden books. Nursery of stars. Winken, Blinken and Nod.

Kipling has a theory about how the alphabet was made, as told to Taffimai Metallumai, Best Beloved, by her father, in the *Just So Stories.* Letters spear-written on the earth.

Cahiers d'exercise. Lined notebook with pink margin. Faint blue lines sans serif. Vanish through a rabbit hole. Take a blessing from the lion.

Find a page that does not tear the retina. Paul Éluard's love poems. Poems that enter like slivers of glass.

In the burned libraries everything is winged and dreaming. *Soirs volés. Nuits blanches.* We are not all born with grace. A manifesto of stars is necessary. Words unfurling on prayer flags.

After Auschwitz, no theology.

She reads Yehuda Amichai. *Open Closed Open. The language of love and tea with roasted almonds.* The touch of longing is everywhere.

Click of ruby heels. The letter that begins in honesty Dearest Beloved. After Rwanda, no words. Stone of witness. Poem that temples grief.

She reads Hawthorne. The breath of Rappaccini's daughter—a fatal kiss. Beatrice and Giovanni in the ruined garden, stand in the shadow of the scar. Everything poisoned.

Schopenhauer says the experience of art constitutes cessation of the will: beauty wipes the slate clean.

The nape of her neck bent over the page. The heart is the toughest part of the body. Tenderness is in the hands. Door opening as the palm of the eye. Claim. Repair.

CARTOGRAPHY

I once believed that one word had the
power to change things, that language
was a skin we could inhabit. Now I know
poems are theories, carving memory
into the long spines of history. We are
caught in the throat, voicing the hours.

The poet's exile is pure sound at the
scarred edges of the world's body.

Country, nation, history. I am changing the
story. My hand is moving across your page and
I find the words: *grief, love, beauty, testament.*
Your mouth yields the vermilion fruit of the word
home. Let me die here.

POSTSCRIPT

for my daughter who would be my eulogist

Dearest Rachel

Last night you had a dream. It was my funeral.
You were reading my eulogy. You spoke of my
perpetual claim that any day was a good day to die.

There is nothing definitive to be said of the dead.
But I have some requests for your future script, my darling.

Tell those who are gathered that I have loved and
I have been beloved.

You do not need to speak to virtue or morals. You may
wish to say I endured suffering but I believed
my bruises to be pale beside the wounds of history.

Tell them that I loved my companions most of all.
Tell them you were one of them who gave me
a better way to journey alone.

Spread my ashes in the waters of the bay I have loved,
for there, on the wings of cranes, in the embrace of the delta
and its wetlands, it is always morning.

P.S.

You may have:
my black dress
my red shoes
my pearls
my hats and suitcases

my books and manuscripts.
Make of these things a breathing archive.
Write yourself into every century.
Find me again and again as one with whom
faith could be kept.

THE BODY OF MY GARDEN

2002

HUNGER

When I realized
you never noticed
or felt joy
at the accidental beauty of things
I knew that to love you
above all others
is to know despair.

Memory insists
even in darkness
my fingers reading Braille
the geography of your face, your body.

You swallow me whole.
The terrain of marriage
leaves me starving,
mouth full of love.

MONTREAL

1

Bare restraint of hands on the plane. Airborne love, electric crazy fever you and me so new to each other. Winter twilight, frost and lunacy. Your hand on my throat in the elevator crush of mouth, the hotel suite's French doors, windows opening to the night on Sherbooke Street.

2

Dawn fingers us through the white gauze of draperies. Your breathing strange and familiar. You make me coffee hot, black. Your cigarette inhales the day. On icy streets, the cold air corsets us. My spine freezes. The last offering of the Montreal film festival is titled *Sentimental Destiny*. About a married man who falls in love with a woman, not his wife—their long entanglement with destiny. Too close to the bone, we decide, and choose instead to slip into Christ Church Cathedral. Light filtering through stained-glass panes, angels hover, the hum of winged poems. Organ music filling us with Bach's Praeludium.

Schmucke dich, o liebe Seele
Deck thyself, O beloved soul,

Mensch, bewein's dein Sünde gross
Man, mourn for thy many sins

Passacaglia and Fugue in E minor. Sudden thaw,
my hands clasped in yours, heat rising between
my thighs, the gleam of oak pews.

3

We laugh over wine and pasta on Crescent Street. I see you weep for the first time. It startles me. We return to the embrace of the room.

Uncertain hour before daybreak. Damp bed of love. I watch you sleep.

At Dorval, we are voyeurs, watching the travellers, some jubilant, some broken-hearted. We were both. Our lives of departures between Great Lakes and vows. In those singular days and nights, the snow blistered with us, in the ever hushed and distant Montreal of our dreams. The sting of it unspoken.

The heart is buried at frequent intervals.

THE ART OF TRAVEL: A FABLE

We must have been meant for another time.
We tell each other this as if it makes a profound
difference to the story.

You imagine travelling with me, on trains
the way they used to be, steam locomotives,
long, sleek, luxurious.

I would have my black-veiled hat, my gloves,
my valise, silk stockings with seams
from toe to thigh.

We would make love in a Pullman car,
dine with fine china and silver, drink champagne
from fragile flutes in a leather-appointed berth,

fall asleep to the lullabies of engines.
We would preserve ourselves, shining, stilled
in the glossy frame of an O. Winston Link

black and white photograph. We would write
travelogues of desire, spanning continents,
and the world would be brilliant with our light.

PRAYER

Let the poet have her red shoes.
Let her have her liturgy of wet vowels and syllables.
Let her be the throat of these hours.

CHAHAR BAGH: THE FOUR CHAMBERED GARDEN

She walks in garden paths,
symmetry veiled against the world.

Beyond the walls, the desert blazes,
hot sands mapped by marauding strangers.

Arid dreams loosen her, trembling
in enclosed chambers,

the pure spill of fountains, promises of Paradise
in the flesh of pomegranates,

her silks rustle, anklets jingle,
aching to be the wind.

DILKUSHA: GARDEN OF HEART'S DELIGHT

She walks in heart's delight at Samarkand,
composing ghazals. The morning opens

blossoms—paths of white poplars to the
Turquoise Gates. In blue pools, his love

turns her body into water, eye paint dripping,
dissolving into foam. The key to her spirit lies

in his laughing mouth, masks discarded—
the scent of a king in her black hair.

BAGH-I VAFA: GARDEN OF FIDELITY

The king hunts tigers, takes pleasure
in the ceremony of the kill.

Outside her skin, his pulse is beating.
Rubies at her throat bleed rumours

through palace walls, seeping into
plots of imperial lilies.

In his chambers, bedclothes encrusted
with silver and gold brocade loomed

by beggars smother her. She joins the
ghosts of other women, takes each reflection

with her, checks the glass for imperfections,
kohl-rimmed eyes watching

the weight of him, diamond-studded,
his gold and heat burning into her flesh.

ANOTHER GARDEN: THE SEEDS OF EMPIRE

Somewhere—away from his chambers
an infant girl is born—his unnamed flesh

whisked away to other gardens—
embalms her, cold-lipped, in marble fountains.

Harem mothers dream of sons, hearts steeled
against tiny fists hammering in their brains.

STORIES FROM BOUNDARY BAY, 1997

The path home is the road that winds through a black ribboned
sky, hedged with blackberries, air ripe with ocean kelp.
Herons and cranes lift off in the distance and hawks sit sentinel
on fence posts over darkened fields as I return to Boundary Bay.

I arrive home weighed down with briefcase and groceries,
stacks of term papers to grade. My students write about
Romeo and Juliet, blur distinctions between text and film—
Clare Danes and Leonardo DiCaprio—new heroes to make

their hormones surge. *Shakespeare has never been so sexy*
proclaim the slogans on posters—homage plastered on walls of
teenage girls' rooms. The Boundary Bay girls, my daughter
RachelKaseyBrookeSarahHaley their names inseparable,

multisyllabic, all for one—are playing at marriage in the
front yard, petals strewn across the pathway, Haley in a bridal
veil of white bedsheets, another girl her groom. Sometimes they
do funerals—solemn mourners hurried to burial. Daughters

of feminists spend hours in front of mirrors, agonize about hair
and nails, pore collectively over *Teen* and *Seventeen* magazines
wearing Tommy Girl and fragrances from The Gap
Grass, Earth, Dream, Heaven.

Letter from Colleen—her mother died of cancer. Years ago,
LaurieColleenDebbie and I spent summers reading *Seventeen*
magazines on hot days by the Beaconsfield Swimming Pool.
I see Colleen's mother finishing the pale yellow hem of her
daughter's prom dress, pins in her mouth—tenderly

touches the corsage on her wrist. Today in Boundary Bay
the young girls gather to watch Brooke's older sister Nadine
dress for the graduation dance. And all around us, marriages fail,
middle-aged men leave their wives for younger women,

middle-aged wives take lovers—or find basement apartments.
Haley's mom left her second husband while he was out fishing,
Rachel tells me. At night, the sounds of tidal winds merge with
the mooing of cows in farmers' fields, raccoons scavenging,
stealing goldfish in backyard ponds, coyotes howling in the woods.

And in our gardens, pampas grasses release a continuum
of repeated narratives, stories trapped in our mouths.
I sit by the window watching the night sky, the mother
writing poems of girls, the art on white sheets like love.

SLIPPAGE

One night in June the cul-de-sac is lit up,
red and blue pulsing Delta Police cars.

My neighbour is escorted from his house, the marriage
ended in restraint and order.
His rage burns a path
through his son's small body, across their lawn,
through his wife's rosebushes.

That night I dream a black fisted storm, a lightning
fury razoring the neighbour's pine tree,
its scent in my nostrils crashing through my roof.

In the morning,
the tree still stands outside my window.
The sun rises, offering up
seaside angelica, the air full of anise swallowtails and
red butterflies.

I slip into my daughters' room and listen
to their measured breaths,
and stroke their hair softly back from their foreheads.

CONCORDANCE

The air is a knife—
the sharp intake of winter
frost over Ladner farms
a Diebenkorn landscape
and the sky full of thunder
the beat of wings
hawks, kestrels, geese, starlings
thousand of birds
on the Pacific Flyway.

The continent is heaving
with the drumming of flight
to Asia and Africa
and South America

my heart skips a beat, shifts

a lone crane spreads its wings
hesitates
and decides to stay.

THE FRAGRANCE OF LOVE

Love has a particular scent.
This is not mythology.

I inhaled it on your skin.
Found it in that rosebush

you saved from demolition,
your hands bleeding from thorns,

replanted in my garden.
Today the roses bloom and bloom—

I will have this fragrance until they
open and all that is becomes stillness.

By this measure I am undone.
By this measure I have lived.

TOURNIQUET

Language is a skin
—Roland Barthes

This language is tongued in water—
it is so delicate, a darling, the lip press
of syllables lapped in sweet wells and streams

exhales amniotic dreams, night-birthings,
tidal pulses, schools of fish,
a testament of cranes, rivers of stars.

This language, a dark siren, your ocean throat
speaking what we could not say, a wet song
wrapped tight around the unravelling heart.

NOTES

New Poems

"Birth of a City." This poem is inspired by the first two chapters of Joseph Rykwert's *The Idea of a Town: the Anthropology of Urban Form in Rome, Italy and the Ancient World,* Cambridge, Mass: The MIT Press, 1995. The inauguratio was a complex ritual performed by an augur to choose the site of a city. The section epigraphs are adapted from Fustel de Coulanges' *La Cité Antique,* Paris, 1880.

"Beauty" is after "Summer in a Small Town" by Tony Hoagland.

"Dream." Victor Jara (1932-1973) was a Chilean theatre director, poet, singer-songwriter and political activist during the regime of Salvador Allende. Shortly after the Chilean coup of September 11, 1973, he was arrested and tortured; the bones in his hands and wrists were broken. Defiantly, he sang part of "Venceremos" (We Will Win). He was machine-gunned to death with 44 bullets.

White Album

"Belle de Jour" refers to the films *Belle de Jour,* 1967, directed by Luis Buñuel, and *On the Waterfront,* 1954, directed by Elia Kazan. The Rolling Stones, in their appearance on The Ed Sullivan Show in 1967, performed a censored version of "Let's Spend the Night Together" in which the lyrics were changed to "Let's Spend Some Time Together."

"Soundtracks." Lyrics from "Baby Love" are by Brian Holland, Lamont Dozier, and Edward Holland Jr. and performed by The Supremes on the album *Where Did Our Love Go?* Motown Records, 1964. Lines by Eric Clapton are from the song "White Room" by Pete Brown and Jack Bruce, recorded by Cream on Disc One of the double album *Wheels of Fire,* Atlantic Studios, 1968.

"Libretto." Lyrics from "Darkness, Darkness" are by Jesse Colin Young and the Youngbloods. *Elephant Mountain*, RCA Records, 1969. During the Vietnam War the song was considered an anthem by American soldiers; it described what they felt during combat in the jungles. Lyrics to "Won't Get Fooled Again" by Pete Townshend. Performed by The Who on the album *Who's Next*, Polydor Records (UK), MCA Records (USA). First released as a single (7", 45rpm format), 1971.

"August Wedding: *Anand Karaj*." *Anand Karaj* is the Sikh wedding ceremony, meaning Blissful Ceremony or Occasion. The *Char Lavaan* are four ragas or stanzas, called *Shabads*, which are read and then sung during the ceremony. *Pulla* is the scarf worn by the bridegroom. The ceremony is held in the presence of the *Guru Granth Sahib*, the Sikh holy scripture, written in *Gurmukhi* script.

"Dream of Billie." Italicized quote is commonly attributed to Billie Holiday.

"Adagio." The cellist in the poem is based on the story of Vedran Smailović, known as the "Cellist of Sarajevo," a former Principal Cellist of the Sarajevo Opera. In Sarajevo, in 1992, twenty-two people were killed when mortar fire exploded in the marketplace while they queued for bread. Albonini's Adagio, arranged by Remo Giazotto, was first published in 1958.

"Elegy." Lyrics from "Mon Pays Bleu," Roger Whittaker (French version of "Durham Town"), EMI Records, 1969. Lyrics from "Jamaica Farewell," Harry Belafonte, *Calypso*, RCA Records, original release 1955.

"Give us this day" refers to the shootings of Amish schoolgirls at West Nickel Mines School, Lancaster County, Pennsylvania, October 2, 2006. This poem is for the girls who were murdered: Naomi Rose Ebersol, age 7 years; Marian Stoltzfus Fisher, age 13 years; Lena Zook Miller, age 7 years; Mary Liz Miller, age 8 years; and Anna Mae Stoltzfus, age 12 years.

Metropolis

"Psalm" was written in response to the abduction and murder of Holly Jones, May 12, 2003, in Toronto.

Reading Like a Girl

"Saccade." Reference to "Didn't Leave Nobody But the Baby." The lyrics are from a gospel lullaby performed by Emmylou Harris, Alison Krauss and Gillian Welch on the soundtrack of Joel and Ethan Coen's 2000 film *O Brother, Where Art Thou?* Mercury Records, 2000.

Last lines of the second to last stanza are echoes of lines in Robert Creeley's poem "The Rain." Creeley writes: "Be for me, like rain,...Be wet/with a decent happiness." The poem appears in *For Love: Poems 1950-1969*, New York: Scribners, 1962, p. 190.

"Lector in Fabula." Title borrowed from Umberto Eco's book *Lector in Fabula*, translated as *The Reader in the Story*.

"Reading Like a Girl: 3." Lines from the Warner's advertisement for the Merry Widow corset are from *Ladies' Home Journal*, September 1955.

"Soja." Lyrics for "Jamaica Farewell" are by Harry Belafonte from the RCA recording, 1956, LPM-124S.

Lyrics for "Soja Raj Kumari" are from a Hindi song written by Kunda Lal Saigal and featured in the score of a 1940 Bollywood film titled *Zindagi*.

"Benediction."Epigraph by Yehuda Amichai is from "I Foretell the Days of Yore" (Section 6) in *Open, Closed, Open*, New York: Harcourt Brace, 2000.

"Claim." Italicized lines in reference to Yehuda Amichai are from section headings of *Open, Closed, Open*, New York: Harcourt Brace, 2000.

The Body of My Garden

"Chahar Bagh," "Dilkusha," "Bagh-I Vafa" and" "Another Garden," are from a sequence titled *Poems for Nur Jahan,* on the legends of the paradise gardens and court life of the Mughal Empire. In 1611, Emperor Jahangir selected his Empress from his harem. He named her Nur Mahal, Light of the Palace. In 1616, she was given the title Nur Jahan, meaning Light of the World. She was a patron of the arts, a passionate designer of gardens, and a poet. Like most women of the court, she wrote under the name of *makhfi,* "the concealed one," in reference to her life behind the palace walls.

ACKNOWLEDGEMENTS

New Poems

Grateful acknowledgements to the editors and publishers of the following journals and books in which these works first appeared, sometimes in earlier versions with different titles:

"The Language of Birds." *HarperCollins Anthology of Indian Poetry in English*, Ed. Sudeep Sen, 2011.

"Paris." *The Carter V. Cooper Anthology: Book One*, Exile Editions, 2011.

"Ancestors." *Red Silk: An Anthology of Canadian South Asian Women Poets*, Mansfield Press, 2004.

"Lisbon," "Saudade," and "Carson City." *The Literary Review: An International Journal of Contemporary Writing*, special issue: *Mapmaking*, Ed. Sudeep Sen, 2009.

"Little Girl-Deluxe." *Literary Review of Canada.*

Selected Poems

Poems from these selections appeared, often in earlier versions, in: *Blackbird, Descant, The Literary Review of Canada, CV2, The Windsor Review, TOK: Book 6, Event, Whetstone, Crab Orchard Review, The Literary Review* (U.S.), and the anthology *Language for a New Century: Contemporary Poetry from the Middle East, Asia, and Beyond*, edited by Tina Chang, Ravi Shankar, and Nathalie Handal, New York: W.W. Norton, 2008. My thanks to the editors of these publications.

My gratitude to the publishers of my earlier books—Denis De Klerck, Mansfield Press, Marty Gervais, Black Moss Press, and Luciana Riciuttelli, Inanna Publications.

White Album. Toronto: Inanna Publications, 2008.
Metropolis. Toronto: Mansfield Press, 2005.
Reading Like a Girl. Windsor: Black Moss Press, 2004.
The Body of My Garden. Toronto: Mansfield Press, 2002.

My gratitude to The Fulbright Foundation for a generous grant that provided research and writing support in 2009-2010. I would also like to express my thanks to the Ontario Arts Council, Toronto Arts Council and Diaspora Dialogues, for grants, awards, and commissions that supported works in this collection.

My thanks and love to David Sobelman for his tireless readings of this work and his editorial skill in shaping this collection.

Rishma Dunlop was born in India and grew up in Beaconsfield, Quebec. She has published poetry, literary essays and translations, as well as edited anthologies. *Lover Through Departure* is her fifth book of poems. She has received awards, fellowships and prizes for her writing, including the Emily Dickinson Prize for Poetry and a Fulbright Research Chair in Creative Writing. In 2011, she was elected as Fellow of the Royal Society of Canada, Academy of Arts and Humanities. She lives in Toronto where she teaches at York University.

OTHER BOOKS FROM MANSFIELD PRESS

POETRY

Stephen Brockwell & Stuart Ross, eds., *Rogue Stimulus: The Stephen Harper Holiday Anthology for a Prorogued Parliament*
Diana Fitzgerald Bryden, *Learning Russian*
Alice Burdick, *Flutter*
Gary Michael Dault, *The Milk of Birds*
Pier Giorgio Di Cicco, *Early Works*
Christopher Doda, *Aesthetics Lesson*
Rishma Dunlop, *Lover Through Departure: New and Selected Poems*
Jason Heroux, *Emergency Hallelujah*
Jeanette Lynes, *The Aging Cheerleader's Alphabet*
David W. McFadden, *Be Calm, Honey*
Leigh Nash, *Goodbye, Ukulele*
Lillian Necakov, *Hooligans*
Peter Norman, *At the Gates of the Theme Park*
Natasha Nuhanovic, *Stray Dog Embassy*
Catherine Owen & Joe Rosenblatt, with Karen Moe, *Dog*
Corrado Paina, *Souls in Plain Clothes*
Jim Smith, *Back Off, Assassin! New & Selected Poems*
Robert Earl Stewart, *Campfire Radio Rhapsody*
Priscila Uppal, *Winter Sport: Poems*
Steve Venright, *Floors of Enduring Beauty*

FICTION

Marianne Apostolides, *The Lucky Child*
Kent Nussey, *A Love Supreme*
Marko Sijan, *Mongrel*
Tom Walmsley, *Dog Eat Rat*

NON-FICTION

George Bowering, *How I Wrote Certain of My Books*
Pier Giorgio Di Cicco, *Municipal Mind*
Amy Lavender Harris, *Imagining Toronto*